SECRETS
of the
HIDING PLACE

Encounter God and Experience
His Presence in Your Everyday Life

Veronica Lovell

SECRETS OF THE HIDING PLACE
Encounter God and Experience His Presence in Your Everyday Life
by Veronica Lovell

Printed in the United States of America.

The painting on the front cover is by prophetic artist Elisabeth Moisey, Cloverdale, BC

ISBN 9781498436496

www.xulonpress.com

TABLE OF CONTENTS

DEDICATION

$\mathcal{I}$ dedicate this book to my two children, Dory Dean Sheldan and Lorill Claire Zandberg who are both gifts from God to me. I would not be who I am without them. My son Dory has shown great courage and strength of character in how he dealt with overcoming personal fears and insecurities. He has become a role model to his students as a teacher of higher mathematics, and in that role he is positively influencing hundreds of lives. Dory and his wife Janet bless me in ways they may not even be aware of. I am grateful and honoured to be Dory's Mom, and I am so very proud of the man he has matured into.

My daughter Lorill has been a joy to me always. I have watched her mature in her role as wife to Fred and mother to five beautiful children. She home-schools them all and is teaching them to be responsible, self-motivated and discerning as they go forth in their respective lives, following godly principles and values taught at home by their parents. Lorill has a heart to help and encourage hurting people, and is always available to show love and compassion as needs arise. I treasure our sharing and prayer times together as we walk our respective journeys following God. She has been my greatest supporter during the challenges I have encountered while writing The Cherished Piece and Secrets of the Hiding Place. Her wisdom and discernment have helped me immensely throughout the writing of these books.

ACKNOWLEDGEMENTS

*F*irstly I wish to acknowledge where I received the inspiration for this book. I know God's Holy Spirit within me has been the motivation in my spirit to write about what it means to "experience the presence of God." This is a message that I believe reflects the Lord's heart to draw people close to Him, so that He can pour out His love, promises and blessings upon them. This is a simple, yet profound message to encourage everyone who longs to experience the reality of who God really is, not only in their mind, but deep within their soul.

I wish to thank all the people throughout my life who have mentored me, held me up when I had no strength to do so without their help, and encouraged me when I felt discouraged and ready to give up. These people are numerous, too many to name here, and some I never did know their names. When I was in my early twenties, I was walking along a main street in Vancouver when a lady approached me. She was a complete stranger, yet she spoke prophetically into my life, and revealed to me some qualities and gifts within me that I was not even aware of at that time. Her words have echoed in my mind as I have often reflected on some of the truths she shared, which have ultimately come to fruition in my life. It felt as though my heart had been touched by God through the words she spoke, that I was being 'seen' for the first time. I now understand that this meeting was indeed an encounter with a messenger from God, to encourage and give me hope for what lay ahead. What she conveyed in her words gave me a new vision to see beyond the limiting predictions spoken in childhood by my earthly father. I could write a complete book about the people who have helped me for over seven decades, to reach where I am now in my relationship with Father God. THANK YOU – THANK YOU – THANK YOU!

Thank you to the precious people who are presently in my life for their belief in me, when I have doubted my ability to complete this book while experiencing serious health issues, and great physical pain most of this year. My husband Bruce watched me in my darkest hours when I couldn't even lie down to sleep because of the pain. He saw me pacing the house many evenings, crying out for God to help me, and knows what it took to write this book. I am deeply thankful for the many prayers my family and friends prayed on my behalf, and am forever grateful to each one of you.

Warmest thanks to my sister Deanne who lives in Melbourne, Australia. I cried buckets of tears over the past few months when we connected by phone, and her prayers, along with those of the pastor of her church and their prayer team, held me up. I was forced to cancel a very special trip to Melbourne for a family gathering to celebrate my cousin Gareth Evans' 70th birthday, which was a deep disappointment for me. My prayer is to make this trip in 2015, God willing!

Thank you also to Pastor Randy Emerson, Reverend Samuel Emerson, Ken Cooper, Heather Dow and Lorie Coffin who read my book before I submitted it to be printed. I truly value their insights and wise counsel in preparing this book for publication.

While writing this book, a very dear and precious Australian friend, Mary Christina Lord, passed from this earth to be with Jesus after being diagnosed with cancer, which had progressed too far in her body to treat. She filled a very special place in my heart and life as we shared our human and spiritual journeys together for many years. Without her physical presence, there is a deep void within my heart, however, I sense she is cheering me on as I prepare Secrets of the Hiding Place for publication. In her very Australian way, I hear her saying: "Go girl! She'll be right mate!" Her last words as she drew close to dying were: "Father! Father! Father!" I believe she was seeing her Father God and responding to His Living Presence as she 'crossed over' to Heaven.

FOREWORD

$\mathcal{S}$ecrets of the Hiding Place is not a casual reading; it is an interactive invitation to a healing experience for one's spirit, soul and body; a roadmap for our journey to a deeper encounter with our Heavenly Father, and our becoming more like His Son, Jesus.

Veronica captures the essence of who we were created to be, and leads us through her personal experiences, to help us to realize and fulfill our own destiny. She speaks from lessons learned, and a genuine desire to help others navigate and overcome their circumstances.

Her thought-provoking questions will lead you to examine your innermost thoughts and beliefs; and then challenge you to embrace and experience more of God's eternal goodness for yourself.

The list of declarations are powerful statements of truth; and when read out loud, they stir a resonance within one's self that confirms and encourages the heart. I suggest you print them out so that you can read them often. And as you read the prayers, speak them aloud as well, because as you say them they become yours, from your heart to His.

Secrets of the Hiding place will not only encourage you on your journey to handle all of life's challenges; it will equip you with the tools to succeed in a step-by-step process, with Holy Spirit as your guide.

Now, be prepared to enter your Hiding Place, in God.

Kenneth William Cooper

INTRODUCTION

$\mathcal{I}$ use my personal journey in my books as a testimony to reveal how God weaves Himself through all of our experiences, both painful and joyful, to bring us to a place where we "know that we know" He is real and ever-present, in whatever circumstances we are going through. My goal in writing this book is to help you understand the true nature of God, to expose the lies that He is angry with us, or that He disapproves and condemns us, leading to guilt and shame in our hearts and souls. My prayer for you is to take you by the hand and lead you on a journey, to help you find true and lasting freedom. Then you can see yourself as unconditionally loved and cherished by your Heavenly Father, and have an intimate and deeply connected relationship with Jesus Christ, through God's Holy Spirit living in you.

The painting on the front cover by Elisabeth Moisey depicts a little child sitting alone in nature. She is focused on weaving a garland of flowers, as she dreams the dreams of a child who is still untouched by the world around her. Her innocence shines through this painting, revealing a young child created by God with limitless potential, filled with hopes for her future, and trust that she is safe in her world. This painting is a depiction of an intimate moment from my own childhood in Australia around four years of age, in Woodford, NSW. I clearly remember this scene where I felt free, fearless and safe, in spite of the ever-present dangers of poisonous spiders, lizards and snakes prevalent in the Australian bush. I was entirely focused on weaving the beautiful flowers I had picked from the wild plant life around me, transported to another world in my imagination.

When I reminisce about this memory, which is often, I sense God was with me as I wove flowers into a garland to be worn upon my head. In my memories, this was my "hiding place" where I could be close to God, where He could reveal to me how much He loved and cherished me. I lost touch with this close connection to Him as I grew older, and experienced horrors I could not have imagined at that time. Yet now, I can go back to that place of safety and intimacy with God, because He has restored my soul and cleansed me from all the abuse put upon me by the evil in this world. My journey with God has taken me back to that place of childhood innocence and purity, so that now, I see myself, even in my seventies, as that little child sitting on the ground weaving a garland of Australian wildflowers, free to be who she was created to be, as she experiences oneness with God in her "hiding place".

I pray that by the time you have read this book, you will have a deeper understanding of how important, perhaps imperative it is, that you can find your own "hiding place" to experience how much God loves you; not for what you have or haven't done, just for who you are, as you are right now. All you have to do to be blessed by His love is to make yourself available to receive it. It is that simple. My purpose in writing this book is to help you reach that place where you can enter into a deep level of intimacy with God, even amidst the frantic pace and demands of your life.

Come join me on this journey of connecting with God, which will bring you into places where He can reveal to you how special you are, how valuable your life is, and how much you influence everything and everyone around you, just as you are, a child of God who is loved and valued and "seen" by your Creator.

Chapter One

WHAT IS "THE HIDING PLACE?"

Scripture: Psalm 91:1 (Everyday Life Bible)

"He who dwells in the secret place of the Most High shall remain stable and fixed under the shadow of the Almighty."

When I think of a hiding place, a picture comes to mind of somewhere to rest, meditate and pray, where the frantic activities of life can be forgotten for a while. At times, we need to go where our thoughts can get off the treadmill of having to meet all the responsibilities required of us. There are many ways to connect with God. We can enter our resting place for a few seconds as a momentary opportunity to come into His presence. Wherever we are, we can ask Him for help in times of need. When I feel overwhelmed, I take a few deep breaths and re-focus my thoughts to enter a place of gratitude for my blessings. We can set a time every day to be alone to study God's Word, to pray and just "be quiet in His presence." Once we realize God is always with us in *all* our circumstances, we can connect with Him to meet whatever needs we may have. The only thing separating us from His love and abiding peace is 'us' separating ourselves (by not being available to receive everything He has to give us). We can always live with the awareness we are never alone. This is a profound truth that changes how we see ourselves in relation to God. As we live our life, from the smallest daily details to making major life-changing decisions, God is involved with us.

Our "hiding place" is a state of mind more than a physical place we go to. It can be likened to leaving planet Earth to visit Heaven in our thoughts. In this place, our soul can partake in the beauty and hidden secrets available to all who choose to enter into God's presence. The reason we need this connection with God is not to escape from our responsibilities. Rather, the purpose is to re-focus our thoughts, and to restore peace to our fluctuating emotions. In Psalm 23 King David wrote of "lying down in green pastures and walking beside still waters."

Scripture: John 14:27 (NLT) Spoken by Jesus

"I am leaving you with a gift – peace of mind and heart. And the peace I give isn't like the peace the world gives. So do not be troubled or afraid."

How do we access God's Hiding Place?

We choose Him over and above all of our circumstances.

Scripture: Matthew 6:33 (KGV)

"Seek ye first the kingdom of God and His righteousness, and all these things shall be added unto you."

Entering into your "Hiding Place in God"

Do not look upon your "hiding place" as something you have to earn, based upon your own efforts. In other words, when you feel driven to strive in your own strength to connect with God. In our Western society, we are very much conditioned to be goal-oriented in order to become accepted and respected by others. This way of thinking is an 'outward focus' rather than drawing on our 'inner self' to identify who we believe we are. When we look outward to the world to seek our value and worth, our boundaries continually shift according to the circumstances we face. We don't have established 'markers' in our belief system (who we think we are) to ground us in immovable truth.

Scripture: Psalm 18:2 (NLT)

"The Lord is my rock, my fortress, and my Savior; my God is my rock, in whom I find protection. He is my shield, the strength of my salvation, and my stronghold."

What does our life look like when we "choose to place God first?"

Firstly, ask yourself the following questions:

- What do I consider is 'most important' in my life?
- What do I think about the most?
- What are my priorities?
- What do I choose to do with my time? (Over and above the basic needs I must attend to).
- What do I think about first when I am under stress?

We are all creatures of habit who automatically revert to learned responses from our past, especially under stress. Our brains have been conditioned to think as the world has taught us. We are programmed by outside influences that form our identity (how we see ourselves), therefore, many of us do not realize there is a better way to live. As we turn our focus towards God, we will experience greater freedom, peace, and the fulfillment of hidden potential lying unexplored within us. Each person is born with unique gifts, talents and special qualities inherent within them, waiting to be discovered and released throughout their lifetime. No one person is an exact replica of another human being.

Scripture: Psalm 139:13-16 (NLT)

"You made all the delicate inner parts of my body and knit me together in my mother's womb. Thank you for making me so wonderfully complex! Your workmanship is marvelous - how well I know it. You watched me as I was being formed in utter seclusion,

as I was woven together in the dark of the womb. You saw me before I was born. Every day in my life was recorded in your book. Every moment was laid out before a single day had passed."

It is a tragic waste of the gift of life to leave these unique qualities lying dormant within us. My prayer for you is that your mind and your heart will be touched by God as you read this book, to step into your God-given destiny. Only *you* can open the door to all God has to give you. You hold the key, because God gave us all free will to make these choices for ourselves. When God created our universe, He gave mankind dominion over all the earth **(Genesis 1:26 - NLT) Then God said, "Let us make people in our image, to be like ourselves. They will be masters over all life."** If this were not so, we would be totally controlled by God without free will to choose for ourselves. We are 'wired' by how God created us, to be seekers and problem solvers. It is natural for us to pioneer new concepts and ideas, to live beyond previous boundaries. We grow as we break new ground, and stretch ourselves to discover the limitless possibilities that lie before us. Do we dare to break free from limiting generational traditions and beliefs passed on to us? Where would the world be without explorers like Christopher Columbus, who held true to his conviction the earth is round and not flat? It takes courage to step out of conventional beliefs against views of the majority, however, to do so brings its own rewards, despite the opposition we will face.

I see our "hiding place" to be where we go in our thoughts as we pursue God's presence with all our heart, mind and strength **(Matthew 22:37 - NLT) "You must love the Lord your God with all your heart, all your soul, and all your mind."** When we live this way, we separate ourselves from all values not rooted in God. He "directs our steps" when we choose Him first, over and above everything else in our life. This is not to say other things in our life are unimportant; however, when our focus causes us to place too much value in them, we leave ourselves open to confusion, stress and anxiety. As we meditate upon how Jesus lived, we see that when He felt overwhelmed by the demands placed on Him, He separated Himself for a while to be alone, to go to a mountain where He could commune with His Father in

Heaven. Jesus took time to enter His "hiding place" to protect Himself from being consumed by the needs of others.

Since Biblical times life has sped up dramatically, especially with our technical revolution exploding before us. We are exposed to 'information-overload' which was supposed to simplify our life. How do we find peace and rest, when we are caught up in the race to keep up to the demands of the society we live in? We need to consciously "go to the mountain" in our thoughts as Jesus did, to commune with our Father God, so that we may "hear" what He says to us. We may not literally hear His voice, however, God's Holy Spirit is constantly communicating with us (in our thoughts and inner senses). By applying ourselves to following God's Way rather than what we were taught in the past, dramatic changes take place within us, which will ultimately affect the quality of our life.

Scripture: Philippians 4:6-7 (NLT)

"Do not be troubled about anything; instead, pray about everything. Tell God what you need and thank him for all he has done. If you do this you will experience God's peace, which is far more wonderful than the human mind can understand. His peace will guard your hearts and minds as you live in Christ Jesus."

How do we apply the wisdom of this Scripture in our personal life?

I will give you an example from my own life. I used to be a chronic worrier, a habit that wore me down physically and emotionally. There was no peace in my soul, therefore I had no control over the roller coaster cycle of emotional highs and lows within me. As a result, I made poor decisions, adding to the stress in my life. I can honestly say that now my life is mostly peaceful, because I have learned what is truly important to me. Whenever I face challenges that threaten to steal my peace, I choose God's promises over and above my own fears. This is not always easy in my human weakness, so I claim the Scripture: **2 Corinthians 12:9** that teaches me: **"In my own weaknesses, God is my strength."** We all have the right to choose what is good for us. When you make healthy choices based upon God's kingdom values, you can be sure your life will eventually reflect the fruits of those choices.

What part does free will play in our life?

God designed us to have free will. Our brains are structured to respond to the quality of our thoughts. Think of your brain as a musical instrument with unlimited potential to create beautiful music. The qualities of the music depend upon the player (you). God has given each of us unique gifts to play our own particular 'music' throughout our lifetime. As we become more attuned to God, by listening to what He is conveying to us in our spirit, we align ourselves with the unique destiny He has chosen for us. This is how we enter His Presence, by adjusting our thought-life to the "music of heaven" – meaning, we come into agreement with God's purposes for us. Many of us begin life in dysfunctional environments, leaving us with distorted views of how we see ourselves. However, because we have been given free will, we can change and be transformed by the new beliefs we choose to adopt. We can 'play' new music upon our brain cells as we align ourselves with God's plans for us. As you replace old beliefs in your mind by consciously choosing to think Godly thoughts, your brain is being re-structured physically to reflect the quality of these new thoughts. When we falsely believe we are victims of our circumstances, we are rejecting the gift God has given us, which is the right to make our own choices.

Scripture: Jeremiah 29:11-12 (NIV)

"For I know the plans I have for you, declares the Lord, plans to prosper you and not to harm you, plans to give you hope and a future. Then you will call upon Me and come and pray to Me, and I will listen to you."

What kind of music do you want to play in your life?

Of course we want to be an uplifting, harmonious influence in our life, living in peace with inner joy in our heart. How do we achieve this? We make the choice to enter our "hiding place" in Him. We choose to make necessary changes based upon new decisions to walk a different road. We 'turn' our face towards God and say *"yes"* to Him. We ask God to free us from old thought patterns, and show us His will for us. What are some of the roadblocks we need to address and let go of?

- A rebellious attitude
- Stubbornness
- Needing to be in control of people and circumstances
- Complacency
- Self-pity
- Victim mentality
- Anger
- Unforgiveness

I wrote extensively about how to deal with our negative self-beliefs in The Cherished Piece, which will help you on your journey to break free from limiting mindsets. Always keep in mind you are a "work in progress" – we are all on a journey to learn and become more fulfilled as we seek to understand what our divine purpose is. As we accept our 'imperfect self' with the attitude of surrendering to God's will for us, the pressure of 'performing and striving' is lifted off us! Think of yourself as a baby in a cradle being rocked by God's hands as you rest and abide in His love for you **(Matthew 11:28-30) "His yoke is easy."** It is in this place we are strengthened and led by the wisdom of God to become who He created us to be. Our part is to use our free will to choose God's Way, thus turning away from everything toxic from our past.

Secret of the Hiding Place

Changing your old beliefs is the process of 'dying to yourself' to become more like Christ.

How can we live in peace while experiencing stressful circumstances in our life?

As spiritual beings living in a physical world, the challenge is to find peace within our soul while stormy conditions rage around us. How is this achieved? By making right choices! We will be consumed by the discords in our environment until we learn how to separate our mind, will and emotions from the effects of our circumstances. As long as we live, we are going to be faced with challenges to overcome. As one problem is resolved, another comes along to take its place. It is impossible to find lasting peace from our physical world. How we respond to our trials reveals the level of our spiritual maturity. We can react in our humanness by giving into self-pity, anger, frustration and a sense of helplessness when we feel 'out of control' of what we are dealing with. Or, we can immediately turn to God in our heart and mind, asking for His guidance and wisdom in how we react. How do we separate ourselves emotionally from our circumstances? We re-focus our priorities, to meditate on God's perspective in the midst of whatever we are going through. We choose a "quiet place" in our soul, to reflect on what Holy Spirit is guiding us to see in our spirit.

What are we required to do as believers when faced with suffering?

- We are required to trust God, knowing He has a divine purpose for our life.
- We commit ourselves to endure the challenges we face, knowing God will bring us through our valleys to victory.
- We find our hope in God's promises.
- We seek His presence as we rest in His love and peace.
- We choose to believe God above what we see with our physical senses.

God's will versus our will

We have been given a soul by God as a gift from Him, so that we may enter into His will throughout our lifetime. We are born for a divine purpose, to be integrated with God so that we can have relationship with Him. In order for this to happen, we need to understand who we are in His sight. This requires us to separate ourselves from who the world says we are. Our soul (mind, will and emotions) can be used to serve ourselves, or to serve God. If we choose to live only for ourselves, we limit our existence to experiencing the temporary values the world offers us. When we serve our own needs by placing them higher in importance than God's eternal values in our life, we damage our soul, meaning we are out of alignment with His plans for us.

What would this look like in our life?

- We are tossed about on the waves of our circumstances without a rudder to steer us to safety.
- Our emotions are subject to extreme swings that steal our inner peace and stability.
- We are subject to being easily manipulated by controlling people, because we have difficulty setting healthy boundaries in our life.
- We make unwise choices for ourselves, because we are led by our emotions.
- We are subject to fear and worry when faced with overwhelming challenges.
- We experience broken trust in our relationships, because we place what we expect from people ahead of trusting God.

What would our life look like as we choose to integrate our will with God's will for us?

Picture yourself in the following scene:

You are sailing in a vessel on a limitless ocean where the waves gently lap at your boat. You have a chart to show you where you plan to go, a compass to guide you, sails to pick up the wind to keep you moving, and a rudder to steer you in the right direction. The wind picks up as a storm approaches, but you are not concerned because you know your craft is seaworthy, and you have the tools needed to keep you safe. You have confidence that you will reach your destination. Your vessel represents the kingdom of God that will carry you safely to your destination. The sails are the means by which the wind of Holy Spirit keeps you moving. The compass represents God's direction for your life, to guide you at all times.

The chart is God's plan (blueprint) for your life, to keep you on course towards your God-given destination (your destiny). The rudder is your mind (your thoughts and choices) to follow God's directions. When you are in God's will, your emotions are at peace, giving you rest even when faced with storms, because you have given Him control over your life.

Our soul is the tool God has given us to facilitate His purposes for us, so that we may complete our life journey according to His plans for us.

Secret of the Hiding Place

When praying to God, live with the expectation in your heart that He will answer your prayers (James 5:16 - NLT) "The earnest prayer of a righteous person has great power and wonderful results."

Living From a Place of Fullness Rather Than Lack

The more we understand the nature of God, and our relationship to Him and *in* Him, the more we have to give to others, for we live in the 'overflow' of His love for us. We become vessels filled with the fruits of the Spirit within us. We live with the awareness of endless abundance, because we are connected to God's unlimited provision as we abide in His presence. As we choose to live our daily lives in God's kingdom values, over and above what we see manifested in the world around us, our life becomes deeply meaningful. Even the miniscule details of living take on a different value to us, for nothing is wasted in God's economy. This is how we connect to our "hiding place in God." Our thoughts are the 'watchmen' in our mind, to sift out the wheat from the chaff of our daily existence. This is how we take control of our destinies, by choosing God's Way for ourselves rather than the temporary values of our world. *We become significant in eternal values by taking a stand for Truth.* This is how we build our godly character.

Secrets of the Hiding Place

You are never alone. God is but a thought away; ask Him to be a part of every aspect and every need in your life.

The spirit of lack is merely a lack of knowledge of who you really are.

How do we develop a deeper relationship with God?

As we look at our list of priorities and their value in our life, it is important to keep in mind how God sees us. He is not seeking good works from us as the world may do. Status quo is not a priority with God. Whatever you have been called to do in your life, whether it is raising children, working behind the scenes where there is little recognition from others, or running a huge corporation in a leadership position, *God wants you to know He sees your true heart and the sacrifices you have made to help others.* Whatever you are called to do, do it "unto the Lord" from a place of love in your heart for Him. Do not feel you must grovel or demean yourself to be loved by God. He sees you as His child who has great value in His eyes. What He sees is your heart for Him (the attitude of your heart) as you seek His presence, just to be with Him. Include God in the most mundane activities of everyday life. You are not seen as insignificant because you don't hold a position where the world recognizes your worth! *You are significant to God!* God wants to be included in ALL aspects of your life. Invite Him into your life! Ask Him into whatever you are walking through. Nothing is too minor for Him to care about what happens to you, and what you are going through. You are not alone, even when you may feel you are.

Allow God to embrace you, comfort and help you, guide you, and lead you with his divine wisdom that passes all human understanding. As you do this, your priorities will change, because your heart is being transformed by "being in His presence." *It is in this place you are being awakened to who you really are, as you experience God's passionate, unconditional love for you, yes, YOU!* Believe that you are significant, unique, cherished and valued, just as you are right now. You do not have to change yourself to be loved by God. His love will transform you as you seek to draw Him into the sphere of your personal life. It is God's love that makes you into a "new creation" **(2 Corinthians 5:17) "Therefore, if anyone is in Christ, he is a new creation."** You are formed into His image as you seek His presence, first and foremost, above anything else in your heart. As you do this, you will live from a place of overflowing blessings. You will no longer feel the need to beg or plead for God's help.

27

You already have it! As you live in this "secret hiding place" with Him, your cup overflows with joy and peace that will never leave you.

It is God's love that transforms you, not your own works!

As we incline ourselves towards God, we are actually "inviting" Him into every aspect of our life. Picture yourself as a young child desirous of pleasing your earthly father, to gain favour and be 'seen' by him. Can you place yourself in this mode, seeing yourself as a child of Father God? He loves you as His child because *you are His child!* We need to get past the mindset that we are separate from God, that He is unreachable, that we are unworthy of an intimate relationship with Him. Once you see yourself as God's child, your heart shifts into the position of wanting to include Him in every detail of your life.

How is this done?

Talk to God as you would a trusted parent or friend, sharing your thoughts and feelings openly, knowing it is safe to do so. This may feel strange at first; make a conscious habit of being open with God, until you find yourself automatically communing with Him in your thoughts. Whenever I feel discouraged, upset, angry, frustrated or lonely, I share this with God. I ask Him to help me get through trials, to strengthen me, to give me patience, or whatever is in my heart. Many, many times I have seen evidence of answered prayers in my life. I now know God hears and responds to my prayers and needs. I don't 'demand' anything from Him (He would not respond to selfish prayers). I merely share what is bothering me, letting Him know about some particular need that is important to me. I make my requests known to Him **(Philippians 4:6).** Remember, oneness with God is a relationship between His Spirit and our spirit within us. I see this relationship as a heavenly dance, where Father God leads us by His Holy Spirit in harmony with His divine purposes for us. As we "let go and let God" lead us towards our destiny, we live in His abiding peace and safety, regardless of what may be happening around us. Living this way reveals the "attitude of our heart" towards God.

We are never separate from God unless we choose to disobey Him, by going against His divine principles and guidance. The most common acts of disobedience are rebellion and pride, leading people to defiantly turn away from surrendering to God's authority. There are many negative ramifications from choosing to live this way. The opposite quality to rebellion is humility, and a hunger for His truths to be revealed to you. The more you press in to know the nature of God, the more you will experience His love, power and peace in your heart. You are living IN this world, but are not OF the world. You "belong to Him," and your priorities change from what used to be important, to seeking more of God's will in your life. The world's values no longer control or motivate you, because they have only temporary value. You now have eternal priorities and live your life accordingly. The following Scripture reveals the importance of faithfulness and commitment to live according to godly principles.

Scripture: Matthew 25:23 (NLT)

The Master said, "Well done my good and faithful servant. You have been faithful in handling this small amount, so now I will give you many more responsibilities."

What separates followers of God from being influenced by worldly values?

Our beliefs and choices!

Our beliefs are pivotal points, based on our choices to either follow God or the world. We are continually faced with the need to make choices every day. What is the pivotal standard that causes us to go either one way or the other? It is our inner belief system (our standard of measuring value), which has been established in our heart up to this point in our life.

Secrets of the Hiding Place

We cannot be more than what we believe about ourselves.

Faith is our belief to call into existence those things that don't yet exist in our circumstances.

What can cause us to fluctuate in our choices?

Wavering in our commitment to follow God's leading, and not placing Him first in our heart.

Commitment is the measure of our character, our ability to dedicate ourselves to godly values. Living with set standards will cost us something as we covenant with God to follow Him. Some of these costs may be:

- Our reputation with people who do not understand our motives.
- Misunderstandings with people close to us.
- The sacrifice of our own will as we obey God's direction.
- The need to humble ourselves, often at the cost of our ego.
- Willingness to release control of our personal needs and desires to God.
- A hunger for Truth over and above our need to seek approval from people.
- Self-discipline to set healthy boundaries in our life.
- Wisdom to take a stand against time-wasting distractions.

All of the above reveal the qualities (weaknesses or strengths) in our character. The benefits of following godly principles are many:

- When we take a stand for God, we plant ourselves in the soil of unlimited promises from Him that nourish our soul.
- The more we meditate on God's truths, the more we will experience His anointing in our life.
- Our thoughts establish the pivotal point that keeps us aligned to God's heavenly plumb line.
- Our commitment to think and live according to godly standards covers us with God's peace and protection.
- Commitment is the measure of our character.

Living a committed life requires the qualities of faithfulness, loyalty, determination, resolution, reliability, integrity, strength of character, honesty, patience, self-respect and respect for others, setting healthy boundaries, steadfastness and courage. Above all, we must know who we are in Christ, where our true identity is established in our heart.

Whatever we commit ourselves to becomes the reflection of our core values. It takes great strength of character to remain true to our commitments. Our relationships, career, family, education, etc. are outward examples of commitment that reveal what is important to us. Our commitment to follow God requires us to humble ourselves by placing Him first, with a willing heart to follow His command to live by kingdom values. This is how Jesus lived during His brief time on earth. There was no personal glory for Him as He obeyed Father God. He became the brunt of people's derision and abuse because they did not understand His motives, which were to love and serve them. Our responsibility as a believer in God is to love others unconditionally, to bless them with kindness, acceptance and respect, to show them honour and not judge them. As we live this way, we are set free from condemnation, guilt and shame by following Light rather than darkness. Sadly, many religions have fallen into the trap of setting conditions on love and acceptance. Jesus never did this! We will never go wrong by following His example.

Secrets of the Hiding Place

Commitment leads to success. Lack of commitment is like a ship without a rudder, leaving us open to distractions that cause chaos and confusion in our life.

Live with integrity – be a 'difference maker' by following your heart.

Scripture: Song of Solomon 2:15 (NLT)

"Quick! Catch all the little foxes before they ruin the vineyard of your love, for the grapevines are all in blossom."

What are some of the 'little foxes of deception' that derail us from living as Jesus did?

31

- Judgment, accusations and condemnation of others.
- Looking only at the 'outer person' rather than recognizing the gold within them.
- Impatience, jealousy, covetousness, pettiness, narrow thinking.
- Intolerance.
- Self-condemnation.
- Anger.
- Jealousy of others' successes.

As we commit to align our heart by conforming to who we are as a child of God, Holy Spirit restores us, enabling us to see ourselves, and others, from a heavenly perspective. Love increases in us until we live in its "overflow" where we view people as Jesus did. It is in this place we become instruments of peace for God's love, to touch and transform others' lives.

Secrets of the Hiding Place

As we release our greatest fears to God, we receive our greatest joys!

As we pour ourselves out to others, we make room for God to pour Himself into us.

Jump into the River of Life

While in prayer I saw a vision of a huge river in front of me. Far out in the river I saw Jesus standing in the fast flowing water; He was beckoning to the people standing on the riverbank to come into the river to join Him. His eyes were fixed on our eyes as if to say: "Lock eyes with My eyes and trust me as I call you to join Me in the River of Life. Don't hold back! Step into everything I have to give you. Come, my children. Be bold and courageous and take hold of all the blessings I have to give you. All you need to do is take the first step, and I will take care of you from then on."

What holds us back from jumping into the River of Life?

Probably the fear of change! We are creatures of habit who cling to what we know because it is familiar to us. We make the mistake of accepting our limited lifestyles (including our fears). We see ourselves as less than who we truly are, accepting what others may say about us (relying on others' opinions), thus devaluing our inherent gifts and uniqueness. We believe the lie that we are limited by our past. *Please, do not accept your perceived limitations as a life sentence! Say "no" to these old ways of thinking about yourself. Jump into the River of Life where new hope stirs within you, where dreams are restored and imaginations are awakened!* Become re-connected with the little child living within you, as you were before limitations were placed on you, perhaps as a child or when you matured into adulthood. When Jesus spoke of becoming like a little child, He used this parable to give us a picture of how we were created to be for all of our life, not just in our childhood years.

Exercise to help you experience the person God created you to be:

Picture yourself building a sandcastle of soft cream sand on a beach, surrounded by palm trees gently swaying in the warm ocean breezes. See yourself running barefoot on the sand, with waves splashing over your feet, as you laugh joyfully with the pure excitement of discovery at these new sensations. See yourself picking up seashells and listening to their sounds as you place them over your ear. What are you feeling as this young child? Are you experiencing the joy of freedom, trust, discovery, innocence, playfulness, fearlessness, wonder, contentment, peace and harmony in your heart?

I believe this is what Jesus meant by declaring: "Live as a little child." This does not mean we remain childish as we mature and grow in wisdom. It means we need to 'throw off' the garments of negative, limited thinking put upon us by carnal, worldly values. It means we need to 'discard' all those things that corrupted childlike innocence, thus imprisoning us with lies about who we grew to believe we are. As you stir your imagination to awaken buried dreams lying within you, you will connect with God's dreams for you. The more you enter this special place in your thoughts and prayers, and meditate on what you feel when you go to your "hiding place in God," the more you 'become' what you are focusing on. As you develop new ways of thinking and feeling aligned with how God sees you, you are actually reprogramming your brain. Your brain responds physically, as new pathways and patterns form to conform to the quality of your thoughts **(Proverbs 23:7) "For as he thinks in his heart, so is he."** (Refer to Dr. Caroline Leaf's book Switch on Your Brain, recommended at the end of this book).

The more you focus on anything, the more you become what you are focusing on!

Keep it simple!

Don't complicate your life by getting caught up in your performance and how you appear to others. If you are feeling overwhelmed and pressured, realize you only live one day at a time, and can only take one step at a time. Remember the saying: A journey begins with the first step. "Living in the moment" is one of the most valuable keys you can adopt to experience deep contentment within your heart. To summarize what I mean: *Don't let your mind project too far ahead, so that you lose touch with the value of this moment you are living in right now.* The most important part of your journey to become transformed is the quality of your life today. There may be little physical evidence of change as yet, however, as long as you are "abiding in the presence of God" by seeking His will through your chosen thoughts, and trusting you are where you need to be, you are making progress. The most significant aspect of the changes you are making is the state of your heart and what you truly believe, not how you appear to others. This is why we should never presume we know another's heart. God sees past our exterior-self to the core of who we really are. He knows our motives, fears, hopes and dreams. We don't have to prove ourselves to God! (Study Psalm 139 to gain insight into how God sees you).

Secrets of the Hiding Place

The invisible world is as tangible as our physical world, waiting to be 'seen' by our spiritual senses.

Do not allow yourself to be defined by your circumstances.

Scripture: Proverbs 16:33 (NLT)

"Fear of the Lord teaches a person to be wise; humility precedes honour."

Say the following prayer to keep you "on course" with His will for you, especially during difficult and challenging times.

PRAYER

"Lord, I feel out of control, hurt, betrayed, alone and overwhelmed by this situation; (fill in whatever you are going through here). I need your presence, your comfort and guidance as I lay these circumstances at the foot of the Cross (picture yourself laying down whatever is bothering you at the Cross). I thank you Lord for taking upon yourself all injustices, iniquities, pain and everything I am dealing with right now." Amen.

PERSONAL PROCLAMATIONS

Speak these out loud over yourself and claim them as your own.

- *I release all human control to seek my own form of justice, and I give all these burdens to Jesus Christ.*
- *I choose to follow Jesus' Way in how I deal with this situation (put your own words in here and apply them to whatever you are facing).*
- *I trust you Lord to be my Righteousness in what is occurring in my life.*
- *I let it go now in Jesus' name.*
- *I declare this circumstance no longer belongs to me, now and forevermore, and I choose not to carry the weight of it in my own strength.*
- *I declare I am God's son/daughter, therefore I have nothing to fear, because He loves me and protects me.*

- *I vow not to take these burdens back. They belong to you, Lord Jesus.*
- *I take these injustices to your Higher Court, where Father God's justice is declared and decreed in this situation.*
IT IS FINISHED!

As you speak these Proclamations out loud, believing God is truly in control, you are freeing yourself to be led by Him, whose justice always prevails over all injustices. The physical world we live in is not the real power in our life. Physical matter is governed by a higher Law, the Law of Creation. In Scripture, God *spoke* and life was created. God has given us authority in Jesus' name to "speak life" into our circumstances. Our words have power in them when we align our heart beliefs to God. Therefore, God's justice will prevail in our circumstances as "we believe with all our heart and soul" that God has the last Word. As we believe this truth, IT IS SO! In believing God's justice is established in our life, we live without fear of judgment and injustices being placed upon us. **We stand up and refuse to accept defeat in our trials!**

Secrets of the Hiding Place

Allow God's promises to paint a picture in your mind of what you have already been given by Jesus Christ.

We usually end up where we think we belong.

God is seeking true believers to represent Him here on earth. We need to live with courage, boldness and conviction as we take a stand for God. We can "call out" these qualities within us by believing they are there, waiting to be released into our life by our belief in who God is, and what He represents to us. We "step out in faith" by declaring who we really are in Christ, then we move forward, trusting God will guide us as we journey into new territory.

As we take the first step, God will do the rest!

Keys to remember

- We rely on Him, not ourselves in how we deal with our trials.
- We trust God and believe He is who He says He is.
- We live with an attitude of thankfulness for all He has done for us.

Secrets of the Hiding Place

As our relationship grows in God, worry and anxiety leave us.

Any problem can be resolved when it is exposed to the light of Truth.

THE CANDLE WITHIN

Darkness reigns upon the earth, the lack of light creating a dearth
of all the gifts God promises, when we come to Him in humbleness.
Each one of us can represent a candle in the firmament when, lit by love,
we show the way for people who have gone astray.

Our little candle lives within, awaiting us to let it shine,
a spark away from enlightenment when we allow God to ignite the wick.
His Holy Spirit teaches us the keys to life and Godly love.
Our light within can be a flame to bless this world when we let God reign.

And so, as each one shines their light, the darkness fades into the night
revealing God's glory, truth and might, giving people new insight
by loving them unconditionally, bringing hope to help them see.
We light our candle by turning from our selfish ways to follow Him,
allowing God to lead the way and shine His light as we obey.

REFLECTIONS

- How do we develop a deeper relationship with God?

- Write down what you consider to be your "Hiding Place in God."

- What do you gain by spending time with God?

- Do you find it difficult to set aside time to be quiet? If so, what can you eliminate from your schedule to create more time for God in your life? Be specific!

- Would any sacrifices you need to make be important enough to enable you to spend more time alone with God?

- What do you believe God would say to you if you did set aside a special time to be with Him?

- Do you believe it is possible to connect with God amidst the busyness of your life? If so, how can this be achieved?

- Explain what commitment means to you.

- Study Psalm 139 to gain insight into how God sees you.

- Say the Prayer in this chapter when you feel overwhelmed and need help.

- Declare the Proclamations written in this chapter to help you enter God's presence, especially during stressful circumstances.

Chapter Two

TO THINE OWN SELF BE TRUE

As we make right choices amidst temptations to settle for less than God chooses for us, we step into living an "excellent" life. This is how our genuine character is formed and molded into how Jesus lived while on earth. This is how we live a life that stands out as a bright light in the darkness, separating us from discord and confusion we see around us.

You Are Chosen!

Each one of us has the hand of God upon us, for we were created in His image. We were "chosen" to take a stand for Truth, to use our free will for the benefit of others, and be a blessing for those less fortunate. Our role is to reach out a helping hand to encourage those in need, to cheer them on in their struggles, and show them they are special and valuable to us. We do this without any strings or conditions attached, just to be there for them with unconditional love. This is how God loves us! We can turn to God with our every need to find His unconditional love, acceptance, comfort and peace. Once we understand our God-given identity and value, we have something precious and lasting to pass on to others.

Scripture: Psalm 43:3 (NLT)

"Send out your light and your truth; let them guide me. Let them lead me to your holy mountain, to the place where you live."

Secret of the Hiding Place

God's richest glories lie within you. Don't allow them to remain dormant.

You Are Forgiven!

Do you carry burdens in your heart that prevent you from experiencing complete freedom? Are you hard on yourself with feelings of lack, unworthiness and self-condemnation? Do you carry guilt from your past, with regrets about what you may have spoken, causing people to be hurt, or decisions you made that turned out badly? In our human condition we have all done and said things we regret, causing us to believe that in spite of what we may have been taught about the love of God, we do not feel we deserve to receive it. When we think of ourselves as not being worthy to receive love from God or people, we often have the mindset of having to 'earn' love and approval, to compensate for our past mistakes. Even in religion there is a false belief God is judging us from afar, that He and His love are unreachable, causing us to reject His unconditional forgiveness. We falsely believe we have to 'earn' our way into His favour. A picture comes to mind of a desert where we are lost and wandering aimlessly, carrying in our heart a spirit of lack and neediness, yet all the while an oasis is nearby. All we have to do is recognize the oasis right in front of us, yet we are blind to its existence because of the blinkers of unbelief over our eyes.

Secrets of the Hiding Place

Don't allow a stumble in your life end your journey.

Let 'forgiveness' have its way by giving it a voice through you.

When Jesus sacrificed Himself for us on the cross, *all* debts were paid in full for *all* people. What this means is that whatever we have done, however we have lived (including all the mistakes we have made), we are forgiven by God. This can be a difficult concept to accept, because in our own sense of righteousness, we believe we have the right to judge others (and ourselves) for mistakes made. This way of thinking is a huge stumbling block that imprisons us, preventing us from knowing who we truly are in the eyes of God. What is lacking here is the revelation that when Jesus died, He took upon Himself *everything* previously preventing people from experiencing an intimate, personal connection with Father God.

We are the 'Tabernacle' of God's presence!

Scripture: Revelation 21:3 (NIV)

"Now the dwelling of God is with men, and He will live with them. They will be His people, and God Himself will be with them and be their God."

In Biblical times, the Tabernacle of God was inaccessible to everyone other than His chosen priests. **(Exodus 40:34 - NIV) "Then the cloud covered the Tent of Meeting, and the glory of the Lord filled the tabernacle. Moses could not enter the Tent of Meeting because the cloud had settled upon it."** The 'cloud' represented God's presence during the Israelites' exodus from Egypt, and their journey towards the Promised Land. At that time, God did not dwell within them. In order for us to appreciate the awesome privilege of being the "dwelling place of God," try to imagine what it would be like to live without access to His Holy Spirit within you. Now picture yourself, if you can, entering the presence of God in His Throne Room in Heaven, to see Jesus face to face in this holiest of places. The true reality is, we CAN experience living in God's presence in our spirit while living on earth. I believe we have become too familiar with God's presence in us, taking this magnificent gift for granted. We *say* we know Jesus Christ, but do we really? If we fully comprehended the presence of Holy Spirit living in us, we would do *nothing* without *first* bringing it to God.

Scripture: Hebrews 9:24-25 (NIV)

"For Christ did not enter a man-made sanctuary that was only a copy of the true one; He entered Heaven itself, now to appear for

41

us in God's presence. Nor did He enter Heaven to offer Himself again and again, the way the high priest enters the Most Holy Place every year with blood that is not his own."

We would have a reverential fear (not a negative fear) for the greatness and power of God, if we fully understood His command to place Him first ahead of anything else in our lives.

What would our life look like when seeking God's direction and guidance?

- By choosing God first (seeking His way rather than following our feelings), we will experience more peace.
- Our life will be simplified because confusion will be eliminated as we follow godly wisdom.
- The quality of our relationships will be enriched as we follow God's leading to love and bless others.
- When making important decisions, we will choose more wisely by "waiting on God" for His guidance.
- We will not allow unforgiveness or offenses to destroy the quality of our relationships.
- We will set healthy boundaries and not carry heavy burdens that belong to the Lord.
- We will be led by love rather than by prejudices and judgments of others.
- We will experience lightness and freedom in our soul, with joy in our heart, rather than living with heaviness by bearing burdens in our own strength.

The Veil in God's Tabernacle

In the Old Testament the veil represented a barrier between God and man, a line that must not be crossed. People of that time knew there would be dire consequences, should they attempt to enter the Holy of Holies that was guarded by the high priest. This all changed when Christ Jesus died on the cross, and was resurrected to sit at the right hand of His Father in Heaven. The veil in the Tabernacle was ripped, signifying there would no longer be a separation between people and God. What does this mean for us personally? What is our responsibility in partnering with this divine gift from God? There were many ceremonial rituals performed in Old Testament times to cleanse and purify the priests, before they were allowed to enter God's presence in the Tabernacle. *We* are now the "keepers of God's presence." What responsibilities do we have to purify our heart and keep ourselves clean in body, soul and spirit? What does this entail?

Scripture: Proverbs 4:23 (NIV)

"Above all else, guard your heart, for it is the wellspring of life."

We need to protect our heart from all contamination, whereby our motives are aligned with God's best for us. As long as we place the world's values ahead of God's will for us, we are living behind the 'veil of deception,' meaning we are not yet ready for the 'veil' to be lifted from our spiritual eyes. As believers, we are called the Bride of Christ. In wedding ceremonies performed in the natural world, the bride wears her veil over her face until she meets her groom at the wedding altar. After they are married, the groom lifts her veil from her face before he kisses his new bride. This custom has deeper significance in the spiritual sense; we are being prepared to meet our Bridegroom, Christ Jesus. What must we do to prepare ourselves for this ultimate encounter with our Lord? We must come "under God's authority" in our thoughts, our will and how we live. As long as we hold onto a rebellious spirit, by choosing to follow the ways of the world above God's ways, we are not surrendered to the process of becoming a pure bride. We show dishonour to God by choosing 'our way' rather than following Him. God is seeking people whose hearts are willing to follow His leading, who will allow Him to accomplish His purposes *through* us during our lifetime.

As we choose God's Way by placing Him first in our life, He will bestow upon us greater authority to decree His will into people's lives as we pray for their healing, deliverance, blessings and answers to their needs. A pure vessel filled with God's presence is a powerful tool in His hands, to show His glory to people. This is the message given in

The Lord's Prayer **(Matthew 6:9-10 - NIV) "Thy kingdom come, Thy will be done on earth as it is in heaven."** As Christians, we have been given authority by God to think and act as Jesus did, to call heaven to earth. Are we doing this? Are we praying for others in God's manifested power, where lives are being transformed miraculously as He "breathes His Spirit upon them?" Is it time to include God in our governments, in schools, in workplaces, in troubled marriages, and guiding our children to place God first in their priorities? Is it time to act like radical believers, by moving in the power of God's Holy Spirit, stepping out of our comfortable lives to take risks as we follow God's leading? He wants us to be "radical lovers" of people who desperately need God in their lives, who need to SEE God in action *through* us. This is how the 'veil' will be lifted from us in preparation to meet our Bridegroom.

How do we follow God's will in our life over and above our own limited vision?

As believers, we are called to "prepare the Way" for the Lord most high by trusting Him, by declaring His truths with our words spoken into the challenging circumstances we face. Are we ready to risk our reputation by standing up for God's justice to prevail over men's injustices to each other, whatever this may cost us? Do we speak truth into unjust circumstances to protect the downtrodden? We need to be prepared to take a stand against fear as we step into unknown waters, meaning we cannot hide ourselves from the injustices we observe around us. This is how God's River of Life is released into our lives. We are God's mouthpieces, to bring His kingdom to earth by establishing His kingdom in our personal lives. As we trust God by standing on His Word, He trusts us to pour His River of Life into our circumstances. There is no earthly power greater than God. We must come into agreement with this truth in order to be effective disciples of God, by playing our part in "calling heaven to earth." This is how we live a sanctified life, where we can declare with all our heart: *"I am living according to Your will, Father God, as I choose to be true to who You created me to be."*

Scripture: Matthew 6:19-21 (NIV)

"Do not store up for yourselves treasures on Earth, where moth and rust destroy, and where thieves break in to steal. But store up for yourselves treasures in Heaven. For where your treasure is, there your heart will also be."

Secrets of the Hiding Place

Miracles happen every day; we just don't stop to recognize them as we race through our lives.

Revelation is information that is 'experienced' by us, where it becomes real in our heart.

How can we enter God's hiding place in our heart while we believe we don't deserve His forgiveness?

What is the missing link here? *The missing link is how we see ourselves in relation to God.* How can we tell we are living in God's 'oasis' of forgiveness and love? We can look at how we see ourselves, how we think, how we respond to the people in our life (especially when they don't agree with us). How do we handle stressful circumstances, and how quickly do we forgive those who hurt us? Are we able to maintain peace during trials? Do we seek God's presence over and above what we believe our needs are?

How Do We Change Our Self-Beliefs?

- We turn our thoughts to God and ask Him to help us see who we are in His eyes.
- We start making new choices in how we deal with negative circumstances around us.
- We study God's Word to understand His true nature.
- We focus on changing our thoughts as trials challenge us, to 're-set' old automatic responses to triggers which disturb our feelings.

- We "step into God's will for us" by consciously choosing His values, rather than how we behaved in the past.
- We choose to set new priorities in what is important to us; to simplify our life by eliminating whatever steals our peace. This may involve a gradual process of letting go of anything that may be causing you frustration and confusion.
- We recognize we are the "home of God" as we create room for Him within us, thus enabling Him to act on our behalf. This means we need to 'step aside' from our old ways of dealing with problems, and trust God to have His Way with us.
- We 'position' ourselves to align with God's will in our life by surrendering our fears to Him, and speaking His promises into our circumstances.
- We recognize that as a believer in God, we are the Righteousness of Christ, therefore we are covered and protected from man's injustices against us.
- As we make right choices aligned with God's will for us, by placing Him ahead of our own self-importance, we become carriers of His holiness, which positively influences the people and circumstances in our life.

How do we attract God's promises to us to activate them in our life?

As you connect more with your heart, by seeking to be real and authentic about what is important to you, your discernment will increase regarding what choices you need to make for yourself. This is a journey of separating yourself from who the world says you are, versus how God sees you. As you choose God's kingdom values over and above your physical circumstances and the challenges they present, you are stepping into His presence and the promises He wants you to experience. What does this mean and what will it look like in your life?

THE PRESENCE OF GOD

What does it mean to "seek God's presence?"

Scripture: Psalm 23:1-3 (NLT)

"The Lord is my shepherd; I have everything I need. He lets me rest in green meadows; He leads me beside peaceful streams. He renews my strength. He guides me along right paths, bringing honour to his name."

I see God's presence as the above Psalm written by King David. God's presence is a place of tranquility, peace, rest, comfort, joy, freedom, hope, and so much more. We may try to seek these states in our environment from relationships, careers, hobbies, etc., however, whenever we step away from God to fulfill the desires of our heart, whatever we pursue will bring only temporary satisfaction. In the 17th Century a monk called Brother Lawrence wrote about what being in God's presence meant to him. His letters speak of his deep, abiding love for his Father God that increasingly grew as he aged. Even as a young man he was able to separate his 'religious duties' from his intimate relationship with God, who ruled his heart. He spoke of how, in the midst of mundane, demanding and noisy duties he performed in the monastery kitchen, he stayed connected to God in his thoughts. This is how he included God in the chaotic turmoil of his physical environment. Doing this enabled him to live in a constant state of peace and thanksgiving, regardless of his outward circumstances.

How Do We Enter Into God's Presence?

We make the choice to do so by choosing to "think upon good things."

I recently read an article about a book written by Masaru Emoto, MD called The Miracle of Water. He reveals how our thoughts affect our bodies, which are 70% water. He proves scientifically, through photographs taken of microscopic crystals inside a body, that these crystals form unique patterns according to whatever thoughts we are thinking. Dr. Emoto explains that each thought emits a vibration, and that particular vibration forms patterns in the microscopic crystals within us, according to the quality of what we are thinking. Positive, happy thoughts form beautiful patterns (somewhat like snowflakes), whereas negative, sad thoughts look broken up, as though they have been seriously damaged. One can only imagine how our health is affected by the quality of our thoughts. As we choose faith-filled thoughts according to God's Word in Scripture, we profoundly influence our physical, mental and emotional health.

Scripture: Philippians 4:8 (NLT)

"Fix your thoughts on what is true and honourable and right. Think about things that are pure and lovely and admirable. Think about things that are excellent and worthy of praise."

Our thoughts are the key to placing God first in our life.

Our thoughts are the compass that steers us to "true North" – true North symbolizing God's presence. How do we stay on track? We adjust our thought life to align with how God sees us. Ask yourself the following questions to help you understand what you really believe in your heart.

- Who do I believe I am in my own heart?
- Am I willing to change my thoughts (beliefs) about myself to conform to how God sees me?
- How does God see me?
- Do I agree with what God is revealing to me?
- Do I feel worthy of receiving God's unconditional love for me?
- If not, what is preventing me from accepting His love?
- Am I willing to change my heart beliefs about myself?
- What do I need to do to come into alignment with how God sees me?

How Does God See Us?

Scripture: Proverbs 8:17-21 (NLT)

"I love all who love me. Those who search for me will surely find me. Unending riches, honour, wealth and justice are mine to distribute. My gifts are better than the purest gold, my wages better

than sterling silver! I walk in righteousness, in paths of justice. Those who love me inherit wealth, for I fill their treasures."

In order to experience God's love for us, we must first get to know Him. How do we get to know Him? We *think* about Him; we study the many Scriptures that reveal His character, for they are written to show us who God is. Study the life of Jesus Christ and you will get to know the heart of God. As we reflect more often upon what God is speaking to us through Scripture, and what we 'hear' in our heart (that still, quiet voice within us), the more we will become acquainted with the person of God. As we seek in our hearts to know Him, our love will increase for our Heavenly Father. As we develop the habit of communicating with God in our thoughts and prayers, it will become natural to turn to Him for ALL our needs, be they small or major. God never leaves us, even when we separate ourselves from Him by focusing on outside distractions and circumstances. He is our Heavenly Father who watches over us, to protect and guide us through the mires of life. When we feel separate from God, it is because we have 'stepped away' from His presence. It is up to us to develop the habit of placing Him first as we journey through the various seasons of our life. Our needs change, but God does not!

Scripture: Psalm 89:1-2 (NLT)

"I will sing of the tender mercies of the Lord forever. Young and old will hear of your faithfulness. Your unfailing love will last forever. Your faithfulness is as enduring as the heavens."

Living in this state of connectedness with God is how we function from our "hiding place" in Him. This means we are choosing to 'live in the Spirit realm of God's presence' rather than limiting ourselves to living by our five senses alone. We can go into His presence in our thoughts any time we choose, regardless of the circumstances we are facing. Quantum physics' theories confirm there is a higher reality, over and above the physical world we are used to accepting as final truth. Some scientists actually state quantum physics is proof of a spiritual realm beyond our ability to measure with our finite understanding. This study reveals there is a higher power (energy) behind the manifestation of what we see in our physical world. (Refer to the book Quantum Glory – The Science of Heaven Invading Earth written by Phil Mason – see notes at end of book).

In Scripture **(Genesis 1:3 - NLT) God said "Let there be light," and there was light.** God **spoke** over Creation and it came into being. Quantum physics is proof there is a higher realm of energy behind all of life which is not measurable by humankind. It is the 'unseen' world some call blind belief, yet now many scientists are confirming what was written in the Bible thousands of years ago. A 'marriage' of sorts is taking place between science and biblical theology, based on discoveries in the world of quantum physics. What this says is, the 'invisible world' is actually very real to those who understand quantum physics. It is this unseen spiritual realm we can connect to through our beliefs.

Jesus Christ's living presence on earth, and his death and resurrection at the cross, is the 'bridge' to access God's Spirit in our life. We can connect with God just by asking Him to live in us. What this means is that we can now do what Jesus did while he lived on earth, that is, we can be the "materialization of God's Spirit" in our life; or in other words, we can be like Christ in how we think, believe and live. This is a profound truth that can change how we see ourselves, and what choices we make. Think about it! We have been given, by God through Jesus' death and resurrection, actual power and the authority Jesus had as a man when he lived on earth. We can do what Jesus did as we declare His name, to bring "heaven to earth" and change the quality of our own life, as well as the lives of others, to align with God's promises. We can "speak God's promises into existence" by the power of our words, declared in the name of Jesus over our circumstances. As we pray in faith, our words resonate to the voice of God. We are calling heaven to earth, meaning, the power of God is released into our physical world as we come into alignment with His will, through our beliefs.

Scripture: John 6:63 (NIV)

"The Spirit gives life; the flesh counts for nothing. The words I have spoken to you are Spirit, and they are life."

What takes place within you when you invite Jesus Christ into your heart?

You are actually inviting God's Holy Spirit to live in you, meaning His seed is implanted into your spirit. The Holy Spirit contains all the qualities of God, His nature, His love, His compassion, His power and everything He promises us. A seed contains the blueprint of everything it will grow into when it reaches fruition, however, all this God-given potential lies dormant until we activate it with our faith. Our faith 'waters' God's seed in us so that it can reach its full potential as we mature spiritually. As we trust God in this process, we enter into the supernatural, invisible world of His Spirit. As we "believe with all our heart" what God reveals to us by His Spirit, we enter into His Holy presence. When we believe "by faith," we receive God's blessings.

Scripture: John 20:29 (NLT) Jesus speaking to His Disciple Thomas

"You believe because you have seen me. Blessed are those who haven't seen me and believe anyway."

This principle, spoken by Jesus, is opposite to how we are taught to live in the natural world (the world we see around us). The first step of faith in our journey with God is to believe by faith He is real. This is a huge hurdle for those of us who are conditioned by Greek thinking, where we must have physical proof before we can believe. I find it fascinating that recent science is realizing the invisible world is very real and provable. The more we trust God by activating our faith, the more His seed within us is released to grow into deeper awareness of the true nature of God. This is a constant journey of discovery, with no limitations on how far we can mature in our walk with God. God's treasure-box is infinite, filled with new revelations and secrets from Heaven to enrich our lives.

Secret of the Hiding Place

Faith is the key to opening God's box of stored treasures from Heaven.

How do we activate our faith?

We look to Jesus Christ and follow His example. Jesus had to activate His faith when He chose to be obedient to His Father in Heaven, as He prayed in the Garden of Gethsemani: "Not my will, but Thy will be done" before going to the cross. He knows our struggles and what it costs us to act in faith when we are suffering pain and loss. There is nothing we experience that Jesus did not go through as a man while living on earth. Whatever we are dealing with, no matter how painful, Jesus understands. There are times we feel alone, yet in truth, we are not. As we believe by faith Jesus is with us, even when there is no physical evidence of His presence being revealed to us, this is how we activate and increase our faith. *As we believe, we receive!* We need to be aware that our pre-conceived opinions and ideas of who Jesus is, can limit what He offers to us as a free gift. The more we understand the nature of Jesus and what He accomplished for us at the cross, the more open we become to the true message of His death and resurrection. As we "think like a child," we are not controlled by limited expectations about Jesus. We believe what we read in His Word with open trust, thus allowing God to have His Way in us without restrictions of doubt or fear. How do we deal with our fears?

A movie was produced called A Beautiful Mind (a true story), depicting the life of John Nash, who dealt with obsessive hallucinations of people who were real to him (see notes at end of book). They controlled his life, until eventually he was able to separate himself from them. When he realized he could dispel their influence in his mind, he told them he didn't need to listen to them anymore, thus freeing himself from their control over him. When thoughts of fear or worry enter your mind, you can tell them: "I don't have to listen to you anymore, because God is bigger than you are!" We can then declare to God: *"I choose to believe Jesus died to set me free from all limiting beliefs. I believe I am free to live the resurrected life with Jesus, who conquered all darkness and evil. I am victorious in Him as a child of God."* As we decree these words over ourselves, God's truths and His justice will be established in our life.

Scripture: Job 22:28 (Amplified Bible)

"You shall also decide and decree a thing, and it shall be established for you."

We activate our faith when we choose to trust God's Word and believe His promises are available to us. How do we do this? We ACT (by how we live) on the basis of what Jesus has already given us. We do not wait for our feelings to give us confidence before we activate our faith. We decide in our mind to agree with God's promises for us, and claim them for ourselves personally. We 'appropriate' His promises by agreeing they are for us, believing by faith they have already been fulfilled in our life. We live with confidence and positive expectation of their reality manifesting in our circumstances. We either believe, or we do not believe God's Word. Our confidence grows as we move forward by living our faith day by day. This is not just a theory we expound upon in our words. We need to know we are the recipients of everything Jesus died to give us in every aspect of our life. Our mind is like a GPS that sets the course for where we plan to go. What is the point of a GPS if we ignore the directions given by it? We would never reach our destination without pursuing the directions. The Word of God is our spiritual GPS. We can study His Word, but until we activate His promises by believing them, we do not grow in our faith. Passive faith brings discouragement. We cannot borrow faith from others. As we take on the responsibility of stepping into unknown territory by activating God's Word in how we live, we grow stronger and more confident in our faith. As we commit to trust God, regardless of what our circumstances may appear at the time, we are setting a new course for our life. We WILL reach our God-given destination as we follow His directions.

Secrets of the Hiding Place

Faith is our commitment to believe God, whatever our circumstances may look like.

53

Invest in the quality of your life by being fully involved in this moment, right now!

How do we develop our faith in God?

We are taught in Scripture to "walk with God" – not to run with Him. This principle is significant, showing us our journey with God is a process, not a one-on happening. We 'test the waters' by moving forward one step at a time, eventually growing confident enough to reach for higher levels of understanding. As we trust God more, we step out into new territory, over and over again until we are transformed into the image of God. This is an everlasting journey without end, for there is always more to learn. I find it an interesting paradox that we must 'die to ourselves,' that is, our ego self, before we can be fully united with God's Spirit in us. When a seed is planted it goes through the process of shedding the shell around it, where it breaks open, so that the seed previously encased inside can take root in the soil it is planted in. This is the beginning of the cycle of life where, once the hard shell falls off, roots begin to form so that eventually, whatever the seed *is* will begin to come to fruition.

The seed of God contains all the characteristics of God. When it is planted in our spirit, it will grow within us as we water it with our faith. However, before that happens, the seed spends time in the darkness of the soil (our soul) before it germinates and grows. This waiting period in the cycle of growth could be called our wilderness experience, where we are required to be patient before evidence of our faith manifests in our life. How will this be reflected in our life? When we are rooted in the love of Christ (through God's Holy Spirit planted in us), His character will gradually be revealed through our thoughts, emotions and actions. This is the cycle of transformation from whom we used to be, to become all that Jesus is. This transformation is not accomplished by our own efforts. It is the natural process of the Holy Spirit in us being entwined with our spirit, until there is no separation dividing us. It is in this place we are consumed with God's love, peace and all that He represents.

The role of prayer in this process

Praying is like breathing, where we connect with God as easily as we inhale and exhale the breath of life. Praying to God is not only verbally speaking to Him; it is our heart connection to Him, like waves of an ocean sweeping over our soul. This picture of prayer is as natural as breathing. It does not require any striving on our part to connect with God. It is not a religious act or a duty; rather, it is like a kiss from God that stirs passion in our heart to draw closer to Him in the deepest part of our being. When we live in God's presence, every minūte aspect of us is forever changed as we become entwined with His divine love for us. We are consumed by God's love directly from His heart, and in this process we are transformed to reflect who God really is. We become carriers of His light as we walk through the experiences of our earthly life. We live in the awareness of God's divine presence within us. We are connected to the pulse-beat of heaven, to bring God's love and light into our earthly existence. Prayer is the lifeline that connects God's love and light from heaven to be manifested upon earth. The power and effectiveness of prayer increases according to how surrendered we are to God, so that His will may be fulfilled "on earth as it is in heaven." As we set aside our own personal agendas, and give God permission to reign in our heart and mind, He can then use us for His divine purposes during our allotted time on earth. This is how we align ourselves to God, by releasing control of ourselves to Him. In this place, we experience peace beyond human comprehension. In this place, prayer becomes like breathing to us. In this place, we are "at one with God."

How do we know when we are in the presence of God?

The covering of His peace invades our soul. It is in this place we are guided by His love, where nothing else matters. We become a captive of His divine presence, so that we never want to leave, regardless of the attractions the physical world holds for us. It is like being in love, where you know that you know this is where you belong. This state of living in God's love stirs a hunger in us to seek more of Him, to want to explore the supernatural world of God's kingdom as our faith increases. When our faith increases, this allows the deepest part of our-self, our spirit, to connect with the deepest part of God, which is His love. It is God's love that transforms us, changing forever who we are and how we see life. We develop an inner knowing where we are able to understand people, to see what they are going through without them saying anything to us. Why? Because God, in His infinite wisdom, knows everything about each one of us. As we become attuned to what He is saying to us in our spirit, our awareness deepens, so that we are able to prophetically speak into people's lives to encourage and bless them.

Scripture: Romans 5:1-2 (NLT)

"Therefore, since we have been made right in God's sight by faith, we have peace with God because of what Jesus Christ our Lord has done for us. Because of our faith, Christ has brought us into this place of highest privilege where we now stand, and we confidently and joyfully look forward to sharing God's glory."

Secrets of the Hiding Place

When we are led by God's love, the Fruits of the Spirit within us are activated, so that our life becomes a reflection of the character of God.

Love God, just because He is God!

Scripture: 2 Corinthians 12:9 (NIV)

"My grace is sufficient for you, for my power is made perfect in weakness."

DECLARATIONS OF FAITH

- **I am created in God's image, therefore I am heir to all He has promised me.**

- **I walk in the knowledge that I am loved unconditionally, just as I am, by God; therefore I believe I am worthy of receiving His love.**

- I carry no shame, guilt, fear nor worry, because Jesus Christ gave His life to remove all these burdens from me.

- I choose to see myself as a beloved child who has great favour in Father God's eyes.

- God is bigger than all the painful memories from my past.

- I am victorious over all evil because I belong to Christ Jesus, and am no longer a victim of my past or present circumstances.

- I awake each morning with hopeful expectations in my heart and mind, knowing I am protected and loved by God.

- I choose to be happy and celebrate who God created me to be.

- My mind is being restored to wholeness as I choose to meditate on Godly thoughts.

- My body is responding to my Godly thoughts, restoring me to perfect health.

- I am valued and respected for my authentic self, as I choose to be honest and live with integrity.

- I recognize I am connected to ALL people, therefore, how I think and act profoundly influences others.

- I am never alone in my life's journey, for God lives in me and never leaves me.

Secrets of the Hiding Place

Yield to godly principles to connect to God's power and peace.

Allow people to see God in you. Don't squander this privilege, which is a gift.

THE MYSTERY OF LIFE

We cannot know the answers to all life's mysteries.
Our questions leave us feeling lost and filled with aching grief.
We ask: "Lord, why?" when waves of regret fill us with despair,
wondering in our heart: "God, are you really there?"

Of this we can be certain. God never leads us astray.
He meets us in our moments when we have lost our way.
Christ offers us His cup of hope and His redeeming love
that we may drink our portion, given by God above.

And in our broken times when we fall on bended knee,
He meets us in our deepest place to fill us with His peace.
We are human, as God made us; He knows our weaknesses.
He waits for us to share our heart with truth and openness.

This is where we meet Him, all pretenses set aside,
open to be touched by grace and filled with perfect love.
The mysteries of life and death are secrets not revealed,
yet we can be recipients of all He has to give.

God offers us His grace that we may fully live.
Are we ready to receive this gift and turn our face to Him?
So as we carry on, though wounded we may be,
He takes our hand and guides us to a place of victory.

REFLECTIONS

- What does it mean to you personally to be true to yourself?

- How do you develop a deeper relationship with God?

- Do you believe you are completely forgiven by God and free of all condemnation?

- What would your life look like when you seek God's guidance and direction on a continual basis?

- How can we follow God's will in our life in a practical way?

- How do we change our negative self-beliefs?

- What does it mean to you to seek the presence of God? How would this affect your circumstances?

- How do you believe God sees you? Write down what He reveals to you (refer to the questions in this chapter to help you gain deeper insight as you journal your thoughts).

- Explain what you believe prayer is.

- How does prayer help us to draw closer to God?

- How do we activate our faith?

- Speak aloud the Declarations of Faith in this chapter and claim them for yourself personally.

Chapter Three

SET YOUR MIND

What does it mean to "set your mind?"

Scripture: Romans 8:5-6 (NIV)

"Those who live according to the sinful nature have their minds set on what that nature desires; but those who live in accordance with the Spirit have their minds set on what the Spirit desires."

*B*ecause we have been given free will by God, we have the choice to either set our mind on what our flesh desires, or to set our mind on God's Spirit living within us. When we think and speak the Word of God, the physical universe around us is energized and transformed by the power of the Holy Spirit. This is how we can change our personal circumstances and powerfully influence the world around us, as we live our life according to the above Scripture. We "set our mind" on God and He does the rest. There is no striving in our own strength, no fear or worry, no anxiety, just 'trust' in Him as we set our mind on His truths. I heard a beautiful description of how God is ever-present in our life. (The Word of God is perpetually singing over our universe as His Spirit hovers over all Creation) **(Zephaniah 3:17 - NLT) "He will rejoice over you with great gladness. With His love, He will calm all your fears. He will exalt over you by singing a happy song."**

Secrets of the Hiding Place

How you perceive your problems governs how big they are to you.

God ministers to us through the whirlwind of our painful circumstances.

How Do We "Experience" God?

Firstly, we meditate on who He is and study His character in Scripture. By meditating, I mean we focus our thoughts to "experience" God's presence as we would a cherished friend. We get to know Him in our heart as well as our mind. Through meditating upon God, we enter into intimate connection with Him, until we become entwined with Him in our heart as a close friend. We build relationship with Him in our thoughts and feelings, establishing trust as we do when nurturing a new friendship in our life.

Our Mind Replays the Memories Stored in Our Heart

Secondly, we choose to be obedient to what God is revealing to us. This means, we humble ourselves to follow our spiritual destiny, by turning away from old mindsets and beliefs from our past. We re-set our brain by turning our focus to align with God's will for us.

Living in the 'Now' Moment Means to be Present to Your Real Self

Thirdly, we commit to being truthful to ourselves, by connecting to our heart and exploring who we are as a spiritual being. We 'allow' ourselves to be vulnerable enough to risk stepping away from conventional values, as we choose to move forward into the presence of God and His kingdom.

What is our personal responsibility (our role) in drawing closer to God's presence in our life?

In every relationship, trust has to be earned. What does it take to build trust between people? Commitment is the key to opening doors of trust in relationships. As we seek a closer connection to God, we need to ask ourselves: How committed am I to building a long-lasting bond with Father God? Am I prepared to make personal sacrifices to build trust with Him? Trust is built by being honest at all times, with a willingness to place the person we are in relationship with ahead of our own needs. True commitment is the same as a covenant. Covenant is like a marriage contract, where we promise to be faithful, to honour and cherish our partner in good times and also through difficult times. When we accept Jesus into our heart, we have made a covenant with Him to follow God's kingdom principles, and place Him first in our heart. We make the choice to partner with Jesus in our beliefs, and in what we think and how we live. As in all relationships, we are tested along the way as we endeavour to remain true to our original commitment. No-one is exempt from this testing process.

In Scripture, King David was profoundly tested in his commitment to serve God when his best friend, King Saul, betrayed him by threatening to kill him. He spent years hiding in caves to protect himself from King Saul. Later on, when King David ruled Israel, his people rebelled against him. His armies turned on him when battles were lost. Surely David must have thought: Where are you God in all this persecution? Yet, through all this testing he remained true to God in his heart. This is the kind of commitment we need to hold towards God, regardless of what our circumstances may look like. When we go through trials, we either weaken in our resolve to remain faithful to God, or we grow stronger in our character. How we handle our trials reveals how committed we are to 'staying on course,' trusting that God will bring a good outcome in the end. As we commit to remaining faithful, believing God is in control "all the time," we become true disciples of God's kingdom values.

What is the True Condition of Your Heart?

Ask yourself the following questions to reveal whether there are hidden, unresolved issues buried so deep in your heart, you may be in denial they exist.

- Are you easily offended?
- Are you quick to defend yourself when others criticize you?

- Do you re-play old offenses in your mind from the past?
- Is it overly important to you that people think well of you?
- Are you impatient when people get in your way, slow you down, or disrupt plans you have made?
- Is your peace easily disturbed by the behavior of others?
- Does your inner security depend upon making long-range plans?
- Do you get upset when these plans are delayed by unforeseen circumstances?
- Are you a perfectionist who needs to be in control of people and events in your life?
- Is it difficult for you to forgive others?
- Are you impatient by nature?
- Do you have deep-seated fears that steal your peace?
- Are you hard on yourself and others?

If you see yourself in any of the above questions, it is likely you are holding onto old offenses or unforgiveness from the past. By not 'releasing' these issues of the heart to God, you are hurting yourself physically, emotionally and spiritually. Why? Because hidden pain is a toxic substance that erodes the soul. You cannot experience true freedom until all hidden pain is brought into the light of God's truth, which is a healing balm to the soul. *Are you willing to stop protecting your pride, and allow God into the deep issues of your heart, by asking Him to reveal whatever toxic memories have been imprinted upon your soul?* If you are willing to be truly honest with God, He will help you release every hidden issue that has caused you pain. The change that needs to take place within you is a willingness to surrender yourself to God's process of healing.

How is this done?

Scripture: 2 Peter 3:9 (NIV)

"The Lord is not slow in keeping His promise, as some understand slowness. He is patient with you, not wanting anyone to perish, but everyone to come to repentance."

What does this mean? As you turn your heart towards God with an attitude of humility, giving Him permission to reveal any hidden pain in your heart, you are taking the first step towards healing. *Repentance involves surrendering your old ways of dealing with painful memories to God.* By doing this, you are "giving Him permission" to act on your behalf as you release old mindsets to Him. When you repent, you are choosing to get out of God's way by "making room" for Him in your heart and soul. As you do this, God will shine His healing light of Truth and Wisdom into the dark places of your soul, thus cleansing you from the chains of bondages (painful memories and false beliefs about yourself) that have held you a prisoner in the past.

Secrets of the Hiding Place

When we live our life knowing we are loved and valued by God, we carry within us a new authority and confidence that attracts blessings and favour to us.

As we respect ourselves, others respect us.

People may hurt us, and circumstances overwhelm us, but WE decide how we react to outside influences.

Nothing can destroy us unless we allow it to do so!

Yes, our life can be chaotic and hugely challenging at times, and our feelings are of course affected, for we are human. However, we have been given the key to "enter God's Holy Kingdom" any time we choose. The door to God's heart is always open! We enter this door through the thoughts we think and our heart beliefs about who God really is. As we seek Him with a hunger to know His character, He speaks to our heart to reveal how much we are loved and cherished by Him.

Scripture: 2 Corinthians 10:5 (NIV)

"We demolish arguments and every pretension that sets itself up against the knowledge of God, and we take captive every thought to make it obedient to Christ."

Our thoughts and words reflect how we see ourselves!

How do we react when something shocks us; for example, when we experience a very close potential accident or a near miss from tragedy? What do we speak when someone is angry with us and makes false accusations about our character? When we don't have time to think about how we should react, whatever comes out of our mouth reveals the true condition of our heart. None of us are perfect and we will make mistakes, however, when tested, this is an opportunity to see where we need to align our thoughts with God's thoughts about us. We are all "a work in progress" and thank God for that. As we choose God's ways over our old ways of dealing with stress and challenges, we "open the door" to receive more of His grace and blessings in our everyday life. It is a gentle and respectful process. He is always "but a thought away" when we choose to call on Him, by including Him in every aspect of our life.

I love it when my grandchildren include me in whatever is occurring in their lives. I feel honoured and grateful that they love me enough to share something important with me. This is how Father God feels about us, His children. I am sure He experiences great delight when we acknowledge His presence in any way we choose, be it praying, meditating on His Word, worshiping Him through music or praising Him in words. What do you think? This is a natural process that happens as we include God in every area of our life. I see living this way as waves from the ocean splashing upon the sands of our lives, a constant flow of blessings pouring over us which never ceases, an eternal process of love flowing from God to us. So natural! So beautiful! So life giving! So encouraging!

Scriptures: Proverbs 16:15 (NLT)

"When the King smiles, there is life; His favour refreshes like a gentle rain."

Psalm 89:14-15 (NLT)

"Your throne is founded on two strong pillars - righteousness and justice. Unfailing love and truth walk before you as attendants. Happy are those who hear the joyful call to worship, for they will walk in the light of your presence Lord."

Secret of the Hiding Place

Listen to your heart! It holds the key to you becoming all you can be.

THE HIDING PLACE

My hiding place is where I go to ease the pain within my soul.
A place of peace from worldly cares where I can go and meet God there.
And as I choose to be with Him, the Light of God will enter in,
revealing burdens in my heart as I release and step apart
from all the stresses in my life, when I come to Him as a little child.

My hiding place is where God speaks to reveal why He made me so unique.
I know that I am safe with Him as I take His hand to lead me in
the darkness when I lose my way, as life unfolds and I go astray.
My hiding place is serenity that calms my soul and brings me peace
to carry on with courage anew, abiding in God's holy Truth.

In my hiding place I open my heart to be with God in His embrace,
knowing I am 'seen' by Him as His little child in His kingdom.
This is where I want to be for now and all eternity,
just to be with Him alone as a child of God where I know I'm home.
Thank you Lord for intimacy with my Papa God who is life to me.

REFLECTIONS

- What does it mean to "set your mind?" Describe the benefits of establishing positive mindsets.

- How do we "experience" God?

- Are you able to trust God and release your fears to Him?

- Describe what 'commitment' means to you.

- What is our personal responsibility in drawing close to God's presence?

- What do you believe is the true condition of your heart regarding God and how you see yourself? Study the questions written in this chapter and be honest and objective with your answers.

- Are you open and willing to be vulnerable enough to listen to God regarding what needs to be changed in yourself? (Journal what God is revealing to you about what you can release to Him that will help you draw closer to Him).

- What blessings come from God when we release our burdens to Him?

- What part do our thoughts and spoken words play in the quality of our circumstances?

Chapter Four

THE CULTURE OF HONOUR

WE ARE COMMISSIONED BY GOD TO
LOVE OTHERS UNCONDITIONALLY

Scripture: Deuteronomy 6:5-6 (NLT)

"You must love the Lord your God with all your heart, with all your soul, with all your strength. And you must commit yourselves wholeheartedly to the commands I am giving you today."

What is the "culture of honour?" Honour means high respect for others, living to what is considered right in principle, nobleness of thought, and recognition of acts that bring distinction. We all influence each other, whether we realize this or not. This revelation has profoundly changed how I look at people, because now I know my life is not 'all about me' as I make choices, either positive or negative. We all have a responsibility towards not only ourselves, but to the people we encounter throughout our life. Therefore, how we think, behave, what we believe and the choices we make affect the quality of our relationships. The people we meet may not know consciously what we are thinking about them, yet they do sense our thoughts instinctively. Most of us have experienced this in some way. We "get an impression" from someone even before they speak to us. We are either drawn to or repelled by people we meet. The more we 'listen' to our inner voice, which is God's Holy Spirit within us, the more we are guided in the decisions we make. As we develop our belief system to come into agreement with who we are in God, the greater influence we activate in our own life, and the lives of those we connect with. We live *from* the knowledge that our life is a unique part of God's Creation. As we "step into who we were created to be" in the bigger picture, we are consciously connecting to God's divine plan for us throughout our lifetime. When we do this, we see the value in other people and how we are intertwined with them at a sub-conscious level. The "culture of honour" is seeking the gold in people's hearts, realizing there is goodness in everyone, as well as the need to be loved and accepted. This need to be loved is what drives us to do whatever we believe will fulfill this deep desire within us.

Happiness is achieved by being connected to our "inner self," our God-given identity

As we become aware of who we are in Christ, and how much our Creator loves us unconditionally, we live *from* the knowledge that we are established and grounded in fundamental values that connect us to what is *really* important. We see people differently than we used to. We look at them from a spiritual perspective, which helps us to value what is within their soul, thus 'calling out' their real self. We are able to see them with our "spiritual eyes" through our intuition, enabling us to look beyond what we see physically in them. To put it in simple terms, *God is love*, and it is love that joins us all together. The power of love is the binding force that connects us to each other, over-ruling all religious, cultural and racial differences. The culture of honour is being able to see others as God sees them, and treating them with genuine, heartfelt love, respect and compassion. When we do this, we "call out" the love and goodness within them by looking beyond outward appearances.

Most people we encounter have been hurt in some way, leaving emotional scars on their heart that causes a hardening in their soul. These barriers can be broken down with kindness and love, because inside them, their need for unconditional love lies buried, waiting to be stirred to life. The last thing they need is more judgment and condemnation, yet this is how we often treat those who have lost their way and live broken lives. I often stop to chat with 'street people' in Vancouver, and am always amazed and touched by their openness and honesty when I show interest in what circumstances brought them to this condition. I feel humbled by their need for love and acceptance, and their gratitude when some kindness is shown to them. Recently I saw a News Broadcast explaining what the Vancouver Police Force is doing to help the street people. They are available twenty-four hours a day, but especially throughout the evenings when they watch for people lying on the streets, offering them warm blankets or coats, and checking to see if they need medical help. The shelters are often full, especially in our cold winters, so there is always an overflow of people living on the streets. There is more that needs to be done of course, yet we can each do our part to help someone in need, even if it is just to chat with them. This is living the "culture of honour," by reaching out to those in need and connecting with them at a heart level.

I like to think that as we look for the best in others, we "step into" the flow of the River of Life, meaning we connect to the heart of God as we choose to be a blessing, especially to people in dire need. As we bless someone, even in a small way, we are sowing seeds of love that bring their own reward, by hopefully making their day a little happier. My husband and I experienced this recently as we took a bus to catch a ferry to Vancouver Island. It was an especially crowded bus with people pushing, shoving and generally being rude. It was tempting to get upset and irritated with them, yet something occurred which changed the atmosphere, at least for us. My husband is 89 years of age, and children were sitting in the seats allotted to seniors. I asked one child to give up his seat for my husband, which he begrudgingly did. A young couple boarded and stood in front of where my husband was sitting, and he could see the woman was having some problems. He gave his seat up for her to sit down, and her husband shared that she was pregnant and was in pain. None of the younger people sitting around us offered my husband their seat after he stood up, but that didn't matter. He felt blessed by being able to help someone in need, and they were truly grateful. This example shows me that we always have choices as to how we react, even when people are rude and disrespectful to us. We are choosing to not sow seeds of dishonor by reacting negatively to others' behavior. We are not judges of others – God is! We stay in

God's favour by honouring people, even when we may not feel they deserve it. We can do this by seeking ways to bless them and make their day a little brighter. This may be by doing something thoughtful for them, giving sincere compliments, being kind, encouraging them and showing them love without expecting results for ourselves.

Secret of the Hiding Place

Honouring others releases God's commanded blessings into our life, and the lives of those we touch in a godly way.

Scripture: Romans 12:9-10 (NLT)

"Don't just pretend that you love others. Really love them. Stand on the side of the good. Love each other with genuine affection, and take delight in honouring each other."

Applying the principles of God in how we live

One of the most basic principles we are taught in Scripture is to honour others. This is taught in all four Gospels, signifying how fundamental it is to treat people as God would have us treat them. Why should we do this? Firstly, because it is godly to do so, and we are always blessed by following the leading of God. Also, in honouring others we are following another godly principle, which is "as you sow, so shall you reap."

Scripture: Luke 6:38 (NLT)

"If you give, you will receive. Your gift will return to you in full measure, pressed down, shaken together to make room for more, and running over. Whatever measure you use in giving – large or small – it will be used to measure what is given back to you."

Honouring others is not natural to us, particularly if we have been mistreated in our past, especially by those who had authority in our life. However, this does not negate the need to show respect to people presently in our life. Scripture tells us to honour our father and mother as a godly principle **(Ephesians 6:2).** We certainly cannot do this in our own strength if our parents neglected or abused us in any way, yet we can make the choice to forgive them and release them to God in our prayers. We can give thanks that they are, or were (if they are no longer with us), our earthly parents and did the best they knew how for us. If our parents are still alive, we can choose to bless them with acts of kindness. We are taught by God to "give thanks in all circumstances," which brings us into a place spiritually where God can act on our behalf to bless us. This same principle applies to everyone in our life, particularly those in authority, including our pastor, prime minister, teacher or employer. To honour means to show respect, and we show respect by seeing the best in others. As we expect the best from them, without judgment, we are establishing a higher level of what we will attract to ourselves in these relationships, incorporating the law of "sowing and reaping" by how we act towards the people in our life.

While I have been writing this book, history is being made with the passing of Nelson Mandela in South Africa. He is called Madiba by the African people who, along with most of the world, revere who he was and what he stood for by how he lived his life. He was an ordinary man who rose to greatness through the extreme hardships he experienced because of his dream to end apartheid, a dream he never let die, even as he was persecuted in prison for twenty-seven years. He may have been a prisoner physically, yet his spirit shone brightly, so much so that he powerfully influenced the move to end apartheid, even from his prison cell. His dignity grew, as did his humility in the confines of prison, preparing him for the role of presidency in South Africa when he was released from prison. He formed a policy called Truth and Reconciliation to bring about peace and forgiveness between the white and black populations, and he actually met with the judge who had previously condemned him to death to forgive him, face to face, so many years after his trial. We cannot begin to know the sufferings of this great human being, and he didn't focus on them. His vision was to free the black population, to give them the right to vote for their own chosen leaders, and he achieved this vision. Yet, even as he was elected president, he emanated a humble, kind and forgiving spirit, even to his enemies. He was a role model to people and to Nations of what it means to call out the best in others, regardless of what they have done to you personally. He lived the "culture of honour" in his life in the midst of shocking, demeaning and debilitating abuse. He used his suffering to transform the lives of millions of people, choosing to focus on his hopes and dreams that propelled him to greatness. The world honours him now because people recognize what it cost him to stand for truth and reconciliation, as he chose humility rather than dictatorship over others. I share these thoughts about Nelson Mandela as a picture of how powerful our choices can be, especially when we seek to bless others in how we live.

Scripture: Psalm 145:8-9 (NLT)

"The Lord is kind and merciful, slow to get angry, full of unfailing love. The Lord is good to everyone. He showers compassion on all his creation."

Secrets of the Hiding Place

Pride is the enemy of true greatness.

God is in the midst of whatever we are going through, under the covenant of His love and grace.

CHOOSING THE QUALITY OF YOUR LIFE

Do you feel 'out of control' in your life, victimized by your circumstances, with a sense of hopelessness?

Or

Do you feel hopeful you can influence which direction your life is going?

Let me encourage you!

For decades I believed I had no choice over the negative direction my life's circumstances had taken me. I saw myself as a victim of continually repeated negative situations until I declared: "This will NOT continue any longer! I choose to do whatever it takes to change how I see myself, and step into all the promises God has made to me!"

THE KEY TO CHANGING IS TO WANT TO CHANGE

Once your heart is open to new possibilities, doors of opportunity will open for you. Your focus now becomes filled with new expectations, like a child discovering shells on a beach. New hope is born in your soul for the unlimited possibilities lying in wait for you to discover as you 'open your mind,' by choosing to explore this new world of hidden treasures. You are choosing the "culture of honour" for yourself personally. What does this mean? You are "seeing the gold within you," the real you, the authentic you, which is your spiritual self as God created you to be.

How does this new way of seeing yourself change the quality of your life?

- You start to see yourself as worthy of being loved and treated with value.
- You make healthy choices for yourself in how you live, whom you allow into your life, how you choose to be treated by others, what you read, watch on the media, what you 'expect' for yourself now and in the future.
- You 'raise the bar' to align your life choices with God's best for you.
- You begin each morning expecting good things to happen throughout your day.
- You choose to be a blessing to whom-ever you encounter each day.
- You spend time with God thanking Him for all the blessings in your life.
- You 'plug in' to who you are spiritually, by aligning your thoughts with how God sees you, and how much He loves you.
- You set your priorities to make wise choices, and eliminate whatever affects you negatively, for example, old habits, critical people, unhealthy lifestyles, etc.

- You simplify your life by unburdening yourself of old, time-wasting activities.
- You endeavor to get rid of clutter in your mind and create order in your life.
- You set aside time to study God's Word, focusing on Scriptures which feed your soul, and guide you to who you want to be from this present time, and into the future.

Scripture: Ephesians 5:1-2 (NLT)

"Follow God's example in everything, because you are his dear children. Live a life filled with love for others, following the example of Christ, who loved you and gave himself as a sacrifice to take away your sins. And God was pleased, because that sacrifice was like sweet perfume to him."

Secrets of the Hiding Place

Lasting peace is a state of mind. Choose peace over chaos in your thoughts.

Love is the life-blood of the Spirit, which sustains and feeds our soul.

A LOVE DIVINE

We are instruments of God, vessels of His holy love who,
in our time upon this earth, seek to know our intrinsic worth.
God values us beyond compare, loving us the way we are,
stirring deep within our heart the love of Christ which never departs.

God gave us gifts, each one of us, to share with those who know Him not,
to shine His light of love divine into the hearts of those in pain.
God's love brings peace into our soul as daily we reach out to grow;
and through the storms that we may face, the love of God will never cease.

He lifts us up on wings of hope and fills the void of loneliness,
never leaving us alone to fight life's battles on our own.
So turn to Him and face the Son; allow God's grace to shine upon
your needs and all your worldly cares, for He will always meet you there.

Secret of the Hiding Place

Love is the true manifestation of God's Holy Spirit. It is the love of God that transforms our heart, not His judgment.

REFLECTIONS

- What do you believe is God's Commission for you during your lifetime?

- Describe what you believe true happiness means, and how would this change your life?

- What is meant when Scripture tells us to "honour others?"

- Do you believe you make a difference in the lives of the people you encounter? Describe in detail how you believe you affect others in your relationships, both personal and general (the people you meet casually).

- Do you believe you can change the quality of your life by your choices?

- What choices could you make at this present time to improve your life?

- Make a list of some of the benefits when you "see the gold" (recognizing the true value) within yourself and also in others.

Chapter Five

WE ARE "MIRROR IMAGES" OF GOD

Scripture: 2nd Corinthians 3:16-18 (NLT)

"Whenever anyone turns to the Lord, then the veil is taken away. Now, the Lord is the Spirit, and wherever the Spirit of the Lord is, he gives freedom. And all of us have had that veil removed so that we can be mirrors that brightly reflect the glory of the Lord. And as the Spirit of the Lord works within us, we become more and more like him and reflect his glory even more."

*L*et me share with you a vision God gave me recently which was very powerful, carrying significant meaning.

I was reflecting upon how to describe the miraculous and life-changing phenomenon of experiencing God's presence, when a picture formed in my mind to help me understand what is actually taking place when we choose, through our beliefs, to enter God's sacred world, and thus His presence. I saw brilliant beams of radiant light shining upon earth; there were many of them and they were pulsating rapidly with high energy. As they shone upon the face of the earth, the beams reflected onto what appeared to be millions of various sized mirrors. As the light beams touched these mirrors, the radiance increased dramatically as the light permeated outward into the atmosphere around them, so that the glory and power shining from Heaven appeared to grow brighter.

Interpretation

I saw the "mirrors" as people's beliefs that were positioned (or aligned) to capture, and thus reflect God's glory shining from Heaven. The various sized mirrors symbolized the levels of expectations in people's beliefs – smaller mirrors meant lower expectations, larger mirrors higher expectations, according to how open and aligned they were to God. When the light (anointing) shone upon them, it increased, thus it was magnified in their lives, affecting the environment in which they lived and all the people around them. There were many mirrors turned away from God, therefore they did not 'pick up' the light beams from Heaven. Their focus was on their circumstances and world values, so their minds were turned toward the darkness. They were not aligned in their thoughts and beliefs to God's glory shining upon them. We all have access to this light and power from Heaven, according to how open we are to aligning our personal beliefs to God's kingdom values. As long as we choose to focus on the darkness, that is, the negative, worldly beliefs that turn our faces from God, we are not 'positioned' to capture His light (God's anointing), even though it is always available to us.

The key of course is our pattern of thinking and our heart beliefs, as mentioned earlier. It is easy to become deceived when we live in a world that focuses on whatever stimulates our physical senses, thus overlooking who we are spiritually. We are all inter-connected to each other, therefore, the concept of 'living for ourselves' and competing against others to find our value and worth, separates us from what God created us for, which is to have relationship with each other. To excel is wonderful; it is the motive within us to be 'better than others' which is harmful. We are 'wired' in our spirit to stretch beyond familiar boundaries that limit us. This is God's gift to us, to live beyond our limitations, to create, discover, explore, grow and be successful. Yet in all of that, God asks us to remain humble in our spirit, where we can be used by Him to bless others.

What are the motives behind our actions?

The motives behind our actions reveal what drives us to behave in certain ways. Our motives reflect our core beliefs, the 'why' behind our behavior, positive or negative. We may not consciously understand why we act as we do and what we hope to achieve, yet we can be sure it is connected to what we believe, and how we view ourselves. We can be motivated by our sense of justice, our personal needs, our limitations and inadequacies, our different religious or political views, or how we have been mistreated in the past. When abuses of any kind have occurred in childhood, certain defensive behaviors are learned in order to cope and survive. These learned behaviors vary of course; some of these may be suppressed anger, fear of rejection, frozen emotions, or a perfectionist mentality where we are driven to succeed (with little tolerance for failure in ourselves or in others). We may be controllers, where everything and everyone in our life must conform to our expectations. When negative behaviors control us, they become the motivation behind how we think and act. Living with unrealistic expectations sets us up for failure and disappointment. We cannot have balanced outcomes in our circumstances or relationships, as long as we are controlled by negative needs or motives.

How do we change our learned behaviors?

Questions we need to ask ourselves:

Why am I doing this? Is it for my own glory to elevate myself above others for self-importance?

Or

Is my heart's desire motivated to help others, to be an inspiration to them, to encourage them to be the best they can be? Am I led to reveal to hurting, discouraged people how valuable and precious they are to me and to God?

Check your inner motives by asking yourself the following questions:

- Why do I want to do this (whatever decisions you are faced with)?
- Why am I reacting in this way (whatever is disturbing your peace)?
- What do I expect to achieve (when contemplating something new)?
- What is driving me to behave in this way (when you react negatively to issues or people)?
- Is this what I really want?
- Am I trying to please others to make myself feel accepted and valuable?
- Am I expecting too much of myself or of others?
- Am I complicating my life by doing this (whatever 'this' may be)?
- Am I following what I think I *need*, or what is *good* for me?
- Am I willing to follow God's leading rather than my feelings?

As you speak truth to yourself about what motivates your thoughts and actions, you have set yourself on the path that leads to peace.

Our role is to attune our thoughts and beliefs to the "bigger picture" which is; *why we have been given the gift of life, and what our responsibility is throughout our lifetime to align with our spiritual destiny.* As believers in God, our motivation needs to be in agreement with "what is God's best for me?" This is not a complicated concept. We make it complicated with our worldly values that have separated us from how we thought as a young child. Children see life as black and white; they are not concerned with any grey areas as adults are. I love observing young children speaking from their heart, saying exactly what is on their mind. When my daughter was little she was sitting on her grandmother's lap when my mother was visiting us from Australia. Lorill looked quizzically at her face and asked: "Mumma Jeanne (her pet name for her grandmother), what are all those cracks in your face?" We usually find children's honesty funny, yet as we 'mature' we would be horrified to speak out what we are actually thinking to others. Of course we need to use discretion, however, it is refreshing to meet people who speak honestly from their heart.

We need to ask ourselves honest questions before we can bring about positive changes. Being honest, particularly about ourselves, requires a willingness to be open, opaque and vulnerable. This is not easy to do, because it involves taking the risk of being misjudged by those who may not understand our motives. The following are some potential benefits that could result from being honest in our heart as we look objectively at ourselves.

- Honesty is where we don't have to hide secrets from God, ourselves or people.
- Honesty is like a fresh breeze flowing through the dark places of our soul.
- Honesty sets us free to speak truth to ourselves and to others.
- Honesty gives us courage to face adversity with strength and wisdom.
- Honesty renews our soul, making us pliable for God to restore us into His image.
- Honesty removes the thorns of pride, rebellion and stubbornness that are toxic to our soul.
- Honesty enables God to use us for His glory, to be a blessing to others.
- Honesty draws us close to the heart of God.
- Honesty enables God to reveal His deepest secrets to us.
- Honesty is a safe place to be.
- Honesty frees our conscience, lifting burdens of suppressed guilt.
- Honesty frees us to be our authentic self.

As we seek to know God and follow His leading in our life, transformation takes place within us. What used to motivate us is replaced by new desires, new freedom and more balance in our lives. Fears no longer control you because you become aware that God is with you always, that He approves of you and loves you without reserve.

What Do You Want To Believe?

Ask yourself the following questions:

- Do I want to continue living as I always have with the beliefs from my past?

Or

- Do I want to change my beliefs in order to become who God created me to be, with unlimited potential and freedom to step into my authentic self?

Secret of the Hiding Place

Our thoughts are the crossroads to success or failure. Choose success!

Scripture: Ephesians 4:23-24 (NLT)

"There must be a spiritual renewal of your thoughts and attitudes; you must display a new nature because you are a new person, created in God's likeness – righteous, holy and true."

Our conscious thoughts are more real and powerful than the physical environment of our everyday lives, because we can change our circumstances, according to the quality (measurable energy) of our thoughts. Therefore, our beliefs are the heart of who we really are, as well as the quality of our life (positive or negative). *We are only limited by how we perceive ourselves.* Each thought we have has a specific vibration to it that plays upon our brain cells, as a note is played upon a piano, producing energy waves which echo (manifest) in our life. Picture a pebble thrown into a body of water. When it hits the water, it creates waves we can see, causing ripples that are released into the water, spreading out into infinity. There is a saying: "What we do has a 'ripple' effect." Our thoughts also have a 'ripple' effect in our life. When Jesus Christ healed people, He used the power of God to touch them. His faith was aligned with what He heard from His Father in Heaven.

Scripture: John 5:19 (NLT)

"I assure you, the Son can do nothing by himself. He does only what he sees the Father doing. Whatever the Father does, the Son also does."

Jesus was divinely connected to God as a perfect conduit, bringing heaven to earth through His faith and belief in the knowledge He was the Son of God. When Jesus died on the cross, He passed on God's divine power to us, so that "all who believe" may have access to God through His Holy Spirit living in us.

We are only limited by our limited faith

We have been given the ability to think, to make our own choices and have free will to choose whatever pathway we want to follow. Whatever choices we make will bring forth their own subsequent consequences. The following are some choices and their consequences:

- I choose to forgive those who hurt me.
- *Consequence:* I will gain the freedom to move past old beliefs that limited and imprisoned me.

- I choose to think positive thoughts regardless of my present circumstances.
- *Consequence:* I consciously step out of the prison walls that hold me back from God's promises for me.

- I choose to live fully in the "now moment" which connects me to my inner child. In this place I celebrate each precious day of my life.
- *Consequence:* In your latter years you will have collected vivid, rich and detailed memories of your life to cherish, thus avoiding regrets about 'rushing mindlessly through them' and missing their value.

- I choose to live my life seeking the 'gold' in others rather than placing judgment on them.
- *Consequence:* Your relationships will bring deep, abiding connections with people you would otherwise miss.

- I choose to remove the scales of prejudice from my heart.
- *Consequence:* New doors of opportunity will open for you as you explore different cultures and expand your understanding of them.

- I choose to believe I can change my inner world (my core beliefs) by making a conscious choice to focus on good things **(Philippians 4:8).**
- *Consequence:* You will attract people and opportunities on a whole new level, as a magnet attracts its like.

THE REALM OF CONSCIOUS THOUGHT

I see conscious thoughts as lasers of energy which, when focused on something specific (a target), become a powerful tool to 'create' its like in the physical realm (our life circumstances). When we look at thoughts in this way, we become more selective and responsible for the thoughts that roam through our brain randomly. When we allow our thoughts free rein by not being disciplined about what we think, we will reap confusion and chaos in our circumstances. In this state we are subject (open) to whatever comes along from outside influences; for example - (people's negative behaviors and how they treat us, media propaganda and fear mongering, stock market swings, world tragedies, and so on). Without discernment, there is no "wall of protection," meaning a screen of wisdom to sift out what we allow into our mind through our thoughts.

I suspect this is one of the main reasons people turn to addictions of any kind, to shut off the noise of chaotic thoughts ruling their mind. Constant confusion brings desperation in their soul to escape, if only for a short while. When we do not understand what we are doing to ourselves through our undirected thoughts, our self-identity is comparable to the disorganized state of our mind. By allowing our thoughts to wander randomly through the course of each day, our circumstances eventually reflect the undisciplined state of our mind. Our life becomes a reflection of what we are thinking, consciously and sub-consciously. Living without any specific direction or goal leaves us subject to the often chaotic environment of the circumstances we face daily. In other words, we are a ship without a rudder on the ocean of our life. Our belief system (how we see ourselves), is formed by how we are affected by the environment we live in. Eventually, our core value system (our inner beliefs), govern how we function and respond to our outer environment. Living this way is a trap that leads to feeling desperate and resigned in our heart. There is no peace in this place.

We can change our circumstances by changing our mind

Our conscious thoughts are not fixed or immovable! Remember, thoughts are so powerful you can decide to do anything you want, when you 'focus' and commit to aligning them with how God sees you. Your value as a human being is not based upon you becoming perfect by striving to reach your goals. Your value is "who you are in the eyes of God." The key is to *'see yourself as valuable,'* so that you are open to receiving God's love, and all the miraculous blessings in His kingdom. It is helpful to paint 'word pictures' to describe what I am endeavouring to convey to you. Most of us know the story of Scrooge in The Christmas Carol by Charles Dickens (see notes at end of book).

This story gives us an extreme example of what transformation means. Scrooge represents what often happens to us as we journey through life and lose our way. We begin life as innocent children with great potential, however, as life 'happens' we can become tarnished by our experiences. Negative experiences can lead to a hardening in our heart, as we develop coping strategies to deal with injustices put upon us. They can be abuse, rejection, abandonment, broken trust from those who let us down, betrayals, or stressful circumstances that cause us to feel alone. One day, we look at ourselves and realize we have lost touch with dreams and aspirations from our past. This is what happened to Scrooge as he gave in to greed and selfishness, eventually destroying the person he was in his youth. He paid a huge price, losing the love of his sweetheart, and the respect of all who knew him. Enter the three spirits of his Past, Present and Future. This is where we can learn much as we watch Scrooge facing truth. I love seeing how Scrooge was transformed from a selfish, cruel, abusive person into someone who was awakened to love, softening his heart so that all the old meanness fell away, like a hard shell covering breaking open for the first time. Joy was released to overflowing in him, whereby he couldn't contain it all for himself. The overflow of happiness, gratitude and generosity poured through him to bless all the people he had hurt in the past. He repented to his family, and asked them for their forgiveness for not having had the ears to hear, or the eyes to see how much he had hurt them. I like to think transformation is always possible, whatever we may have done in our past to hurt others and ourselves.

God never gives up on us!

As the sun rises each and every day over the earth, so God's glory shines faithfully upon us to bless us with His promises of new hope, new opportunities to change, new love, and new revelations to transform us into "a new creation," as He created us to be (**2 Corinthians 5:17 - NIV) "Therefore, if anyone is in Christ, he is a new creation; the old has gone, the new has come!"**

Allow your heart to guide you!

Our heart and brain are connected – the eyes of our heart reveal our deep, sub-conscious beliefs.

Your heart is where your true self abides. Your heart contains all your memories; over your lifetime it accumulates all the beliefs you have allowed to take root through your thoughts. Your mind is the gateway to what you choose to believe. Your heart is the 'collection' of accumulated beliefs that become the foundation of how you see yourself. These self-beliefs establish your core values that govern the choices you make, and how you live your life. Your heart beliefs are the measuring tool from which you operate as a human being, taking you on your particular life journey. This involves your attitudes, the 'triggers' that stir your emotions, your choices of friends, your passions, and your habits, positive or negative.

In order to change your present circumstances into what you would like your life to become, you need to change your heart beliefs, and to change your heart beliefs, you need to change your thought patterns.

The Past

We all have something to deal with from our past, some regrets, or perhaps we are holding onto unforgiveness that needs to be released. We may feel condemned by the poor choices we made, or the painful memories of abuses that may have seriously damaged us. In order to be set free from the effects of our past, we need to come to terms with whatever happened. We have to face the truth and do whatever we can to move beyond these old mindsets, which represent prisons that have held us captive for too long. In my first book The Cherished Piece, I go into great detail about how to deal with our past, including some exercises and questions at the end of each chapter. I will not repeat this information here, other than to say; *"we cannot move beyond our painful memories, until we are willing to face whatever is preventing us from experiencing freedom in our life."* This freedom is found by being truthful and authentic about whatever blocks (boulders) still exist in our soul. These old painful memories have imprinted their DNA in the cells of our body. Science has proven memories are stored within us, and techniques have been developed to release these 'toxic' memories, thus facilitating emotional healing. I personally know someone who was helped by one of these techniques to overcome terrible memories from extreme abuse in her childhood. Sozo prayer (Salvation, healing and deliverance) is a very powerful tool to unblock and release toxic memories. I am not advocating any special treatment, other than to say there is help available to those who really want to deal with their broken past.

In order to receive help, we must want to change more than we want to protect ourselves by hiding from truth.

The Present

The old saying – Today is the first day of the rest of your life – encourages me. It is never too late to begin a new journey, take a different road, and choose new ways of thinking and believing. Again, I refer to Scrooge who was an old man before he had revelation of where his poor choices had led him. Yet it wasn't too late for him to discover happiness, freedom and joy beyond measure. What was it that changed him? It wasn't the three spirits of Past, Present and Future, for they merely showed him a picture of himself. What changed him was the revelation of what was truly important in life. We are faced with such decisions each day, as we make choices in how we deal with whatever we are confronted with. Every new day is an opportunity to be better than we were yesterday. We can always learn something new, and live to higher values as we press forward, with an attitude of openness and willingness to change. We won't always succeed because we are human, yet we can learn from our mistakes as we endeavour to make wiser choices along the way. *The choices we make today are the seeds of what our tomorrows will become.*

The Future

Our future is unknown, therefore it is a mystery. Our future is the unwritten page lying in front of us, awaiting the outcome of whatever choices we make in our present existence. Of course, not everything in our future is determined by our choices now, but to a large extent we do have control of the quality of our life in the years ahead. As we make wise choices in the "now" season of our life, *there will be a positive harvest in the future*. Our destinies are formed by our choices, as we make decisions in our human journey from day to day. The mystery of life is that we do not know exactly what lies ahead, nor do we know what we are capable of as we seek to learn and grow. It is an adventure to welcome and celebrate as we step into our future. Speaking from the point of view of a woman well into her seventies, I can honestly say that I am excited about what God is revealing to me, as I seek to learn more about what it means to draw closer to Him. It is exhilarating to anticipate this journey of discovering new truths and revelations each day. I realize now how much I do not know, and hunger to learn more with the excitement of a child beginning its life.

Happiness is a Choice!

Let me explain what I mean by this statement. My family and I travelled to Mexico where we visited a Mayan village in the jungle. These tribal people have made the choice to live by their old ancestors' culture in extreme poverty (by Western standards). If they chose to, they could move closer to the city of Cancun to seek more material prosperity, however, they do not see themselves as living in lack, for they know who they are and are content with their choices to live simply. When tour guides take people into their village, the Mayan people have specifically requested no-one give money or gifts to their children, because they do not want to cultivate a 'begging' attitude in them. Their homes have dirt floors, and are made of palm leaves and other materials taken from the jungle around them. They have chosen not to accept social assistance, because they want to live without any restrictions that may be placed upon them. Their food staple is maize, which they grind themselves. They do not make use of hospital facilities to give birth to their children. I saw absolute peace and contentment in the children, who do not have manufactured toys or electronics like television to entertain them. The toys they do have are handmade by the villagers from natural resources available to them. The original Mayan people were peaceable before being conquered by warlike tribes later on in history.

Happiness and peace are both states of "inner health" in our spirit. Happiness is the result of peace in our heart, and peace is the result of knowing who we really are spiritually. Our true identity cannot be accurately defined by how others see us. Being content and fulfilled is a reflection of our inner self, where we are grounded in values that connect us to God's values. When we seek happiness outside of this "hiding place" within us, we will inevitably be disappointed, for everything physical is of a temporary nature. Happiness is an abiding state of being at rest in our soul, where our life reflects peace and harmony as we consciously choose this way of living. Once we are grounded in heavenly values, we are stable emotionally, even when unexpected stresses occur to challenge us, because we have 'chosen' happiness as a way of life. This is not a selfish way to live, for as we function from this deep connection with God who lives in us, we have more than enough to pass on and be a blessing to others.

How do we reach this state?

- We change our thought patterns by choosing to 'put away old things' (familiar thoughts and habits), and re-focus on who we are as a spiritual being.
- We don't settle for what we knew in the past, but choose to believe, by faith, that we are much more than our old self.
- We "set our mind" to be determined to choose and follow what God has destined for us.
- We gradually eliminate those things in our life that steal our time, peace and joy (anything which causes conflict in our soul; for example, negative habits and lifestyle choices).
- We simplify our life by making healthy choices in relationships, choosing healthy habits, being discriminating about what we watch in the media, getting out of debt, not buying excessively on credit cards, etc.

These are just a few suggestions to help you 'unload' whatever is burdening you. Make a list for yourself of what you should eliminate from your schedule, and another list of what you would like your life to look like. The main purpose of this exercise is to free your inner spirit so that you can live from your heart as a child, unencumbered by what life has put upon you. Choose simplicity as often as you can. Think about the Mayan people and how unencumbered they are because of their simple lifestyle. Of course we do not have to be that drastic in our choices, however, there is no doubt many belongings and responsibilities could be eliminated to unburden you, which would result in more lightness and freedom in your soul.

Scriptures: Matthew 5:8 (NLT)

"God blesses those whose hearts are pure, for they will see God."

Deuteronomy 29:29 (NLT)

"The secret things belong to the Lord our God, but the things that are revealed belong to us and to our children forever, that we may obey all the words of this law."

Secrets of the Hiding Place

Our faith enables God to release His divine power into our circumstances.

When you believe truth in your heart, it becomes real in your life.

THE WAY

The paths of life are many; it is easy to lose our way
in the mire of so many choices that can often lead us astray.
We hunger for relief from the pain we feel within,
trying to fill our empty void with things that are rooted in sin.

The paths we see are many, easy to enter in,
requiring little sacrifice or any discipline.
There is a better way for those who seek the Truth,
willing to follow the narrow path with a hunger for what is real.

This world can be confusing, false messages galore
to fill our minds with idols which take us from our God.
God's Way leads us to wholeness, filling all our needs
with the Lord's Holy Spirit and His everlasting peace.

REFLECTIONS

- Describe what being a "mirror image of God" means.

- How does this change your self-image?

- Write about what you believe are the motives behind what is important to you, and the decisions you have made in the past. When we understand what motivates us, we gain deeper insight into why we think and act as we do.

- Study the checklist in this chapter to help you understand the importance of what motivates us to make certain choices in our life.

- Describe how being honest with ourselves affects the quality of our life.

- Before making important decisions, write down the pros and cons to help you gain insight into the possible consequences of your choices.

- Describe how our thinking affects our circumstances.

- Journal a synopsis of how your past has affected your present life.

- Now write about the present and what you would like to change.

- When this is done, journal how you would like to see your future unfold.

- What can you do to bring about this vision for your future?

Chapter Six

CHOOSE LIFE

Scripture: Deuteronomy 30:19-20 (NIV)

"Now choose life, so that you and your children may live and that you may love the Lord your God, listen to His voice and hold fast to Him."

*W*hat are some practical steps we need to take to align in our heart and mind with God's promises of New Life?

Setting Healthy Boundaries

Firstly, what are boundaries? They are borders we set with our mind to control what we allow into our life.

Why do we need boundaries?

Picture yourself in your home; someone knocks on your front door. You open it to see a scruffy, threatening person asking to be allowed in to your home. What would you do? You would of course shut the door in his face with no qualms about doing so. Now picture your physical home as your mind. Would you be as discerning about not allowing negative thoughts to enter into your personal space? Let's say, for example, fear is knocking on the door of your mind. Would you tell it to get lost, recognizing it as an unwelcome intruder? Our boundaries are established by our core beliefs, rather than any physical boundaries we may erect to protect ourselves. To give you an example of what I mean; one person can say "no" and there is no mistaking its meaning, whereas, someone else's "no" lacks conviction. What is the difference here? The difference is who they believe themselves to be. Their "core belief" about themselves is conveyed to others without them even speaking. Many of us have had our core beliefs corrupted by abuse in varied forms. Our boundaries were invaded before we knew how to protect ourselves. My book, The Cherished Piece, deals thoroughly with these issues if you need more help in establishing healthy boundaries in your life. I am reiterating some of what I wrote, because of the huge impact boundaries play in affecting the quality of our life.

Our self-beliefs are the foundation and basis upon which we establish what our life will become, the core of where we think and act from. The pathway to freedom lies before each one of us, based upon what we believe about ourselves. Whenever we feel unworthy, we make poor choices because we do not believe we deserve anything better. Until you change your beliefs about who you are from God's perspective, these old patterns of thinking will continue. This is the reason I quote Scripture for you to focus on, to re-program your core beliefs about yourself. As you re-structure your beliefs to align with who you were created to be, you will gradually take on your new "transformed" identity. This is how you become a person who manifests the image of God, which will be reflected in the choices you make, and how you live your life. This is how you live in the presence of God, by thinking as He thinks, so that eventually you see yourself the way He sees you. Not only do you enter into His great love for you, you also receive God's wisdom, guidance, peace, protection, favour, and all of the promises He holds for you personally.

Secrets of the Hiding Place

I am defined by who I believe myself to be, not by what is spoken over me by others.

God planted dreams in me, therefore, nothing can prevent their fruition in my life when I agree with Him.

Making wise choices

In old folklore, many truthful sayings have been passed along, revealing how our ancestors sought truth to create guideposts to live by. Picture a lighthouse built upon a rock to guide ships, to warn them of dangerous reefs so that they can avoid being shipwrecked. When we don't have lighthouses (guideposts) to help us establish healthy boundaries as we set our course through life, we are subject to shipwrecks (consequences of poor decisions) in our circumstances. We see the results of this in the lives of people who have lost their way, who have been shipwrecked by drug addictions, alcoholism, immoral lifestyles, broken marriages and relationships, sexual abuse, criminal activity, emotional breakdowns, depression, hopelessness, and resignation to what they perceive as no way out to a better life. The guideposts we need to base our life on are eternal values given to us by our Creator, those truths that give us everything we need to lead full, meaningful and productive lives. We have an internal compass to keep us on course, however, if we don't listen to our inner voice (God within us), we make errors of judgment that have their own consequences. Our thoughts are the rudder of our ship that steer us in whatever direction we allow them to. The Captain of our ship is God, who needs our full cooperation to take us to our godly destination. If we choose to disobey our Captain by believing we know better with our pride, ego or willfulness, we will likely end up shipwrecked on unseen reefs of destruction. We have been given the gift of free will to choose which course we will take – our own or our Creator's.

When we feel deficient and unworthy, this is reflected into our life, no matter what image we may endeavour to present to the world around us.

The importance of setting healthy boundaries has been well documented by professional experts, however, I would like to share some personal perspectives regarding how imperative it is to commit to applying wisdom in our choices. As we establish godly values to live by, this helps us to enter into our own "hiding place in God." As a child being raised in the 1940's and 1950's, I was taught very little about having the right to make healthy choices for myself, to form opinions that could influence the direction my life would take. The concept of setting healthy boundaries in my childhood was foreign to me, therefore I lived without any sense of control over who I was or wanted to be. Can you relate to what I am sharing with you? I suspect most of us have stories of some kind of dysfunctional habits learned from our childhood. In current times I have observed that many young people are more willing to face the need to set healthy boundaries, to form their own opinions about what is important to them.

WHAT ARE UNHEALTHY BOUNDARIES?

- The need to please others rather than take a stand for ourselves.
- Being ruled by the fear that we will be rejected if we oppose others' points of view (even if that means we victimize ourselves by not speaking up).
- Giving control to others when we need to make important decisions in our life.
- Seeing ourselves as 'victims of our circumstances,' causing us to live with a fatalistic attitude.
- Not feeling valuable or loved (never feeling 'good enough' to be treated well by others).
- Difficulty making firm decisions and following them up with commitment.
- Fear of taking on leadership roles requiring decisive abilities.
- Living as an 'enabler,' by supporting others' negative behaviors. (Enablers 'need to be needed' by someone in greater need than themselves).
- Playing the role of a martyr, by placing others' needs ahead of our own healthy boundaries. Doing this leads to feeling victimized and deprived of having our basic needs respected. Living this way results in hidden resentment that can trigger depression, as we deny our right to choose the best for ourselves. People who have difficulty confronting negative behaviors

from others towards them are prone to accepting disrespect, at the cost of their dignity and self-respect.

Conversely, we can make healthy choices by:

- Following our natural inborn gifts, meaning whatever inspires us and stirs passion to pursue them.
- Establishing healthy boundaries, thereby setting limits on what others may expect of us.
- Looking after our basic needs to establish a healthy lifestyle, including making wise choices in how we use our time, and choosing constructive relationships (not allowing others to take advantage of us in negative ways).
- Choosing to "value the moment" and be fully connected to where God is leading us.

There are many negative consequences from not setting healthy boundaries. Living in this way results in a constant state of 'reacting' to our circumstances, as opposed to setting our course in life by making constructive choices for ourselves. People who are natural leaders have learned to place value in their inherent gifts; they choose to pursue their destiny, over and above how others may or may not judge them to be. They listen to their "inner compass," which is God's Holy Spirit within them, following "True North" towards their God-given life purpose. They have learned to set healthy boundaries, separating themselves from popular opinion (thus risking judgment from others). There is great freedom in living this way, which I do not believe to be selfishness. How can we effectively help others when we have a low opinion of ourselves (when we believe sub-consciously we are unworthy of setting healthy boundaries)? In order to have lasting peace in our heart, (where we are divinely led by God to connect to His direction and guidance), we need to simplify our life by eliminating those things that steal our joy. In other words, we need to prioritize what is truly important to us, by making definitive choices as to what is close to our heart. We need to discern what is distracting us, and causing confusion in our thoughts and feelings. How do we discern what is best for us? We need to enter into our "hiding place in God."

How does entering our "hiding place in God" help us achieve this?

In order to recognize what 'voices' we are listening to, that is, the chatter of uncontrolled thoughts that drift into our mind unceasingly, or the Holy Spirit of God within us, we must separate ourselves from 'picking up' random thoughts. We need to make ourselves available to listen to what God is saying to us.

Scripture: Hebrews 4:9-10 (NLT)

"There is a special rest still waiting for the people of God. For all who enter into God's rest will find rest from their labours."

Secret of the Hiding Place

We are like a musical instrument. When God's love rules our heart, we are in harmony with the music of Heaven.

I cannot over emphasize how important it is to realize you can choose which thoughts you think. You are not an automaton, subject to whatever thoughts roll around your mind. You have been given free will by your Creator to choose which pathway in life you want to follow. You can allow yourself to be victimized by your past, or present for that matter, or you can begin to establish healthy boundaries. How? Firstly, by consciously choosing which thoughts you entertain, and secondly, by deciding to be responsible and accountable for the quality of your life choices. *Remember, you are only limited by your beliefs about yourself.* As you re-focus your beliefs (your thoughts) about who you believe you are, with unlimited potential to become what you want to be, you are stepping beyond the negative strongholds and lies you may have aligned yourself with in the past.

Steps you need to take to set yourself free from lies and limiting beliefs

- Recognize you were created by God to be unique and outstanding, not a copy of anyone else born in the universe.

- Realize you need to come into agreement (in your thoughts and heart beliefs) with how God created you to be.
- Understand the power of your thoughts, which control the structure of your brain, and how it affects your body and emotions (more about this in future chapters).
- You are not limited by your past circumstances and how people treated and perceived you, unless you agree with these lies.
- You are worthy of being loved and valued as you are right now. You are not a mistake! You were chosen by God for a purpose **(1 John 3:1 - NIV) "How great is the love the Father has lavished on us, that we should be called children of God."**
- You cannot love others in a healthy way until you see yourself as worthy of receiving love.
- It is not selfish to value yourself as a child of God, worthy of making constructive choices to improve your life.
- You have the God-given responsibility to chart the course of your life, according to His will for you. Allow God's peace to lead you; trust in His wisdom rather than your own striving.
- No-one else can make these choices for you!
- Don't be so hard on yourself! Positive change occurs when we consciously choose to take 'rest breaks' from demands placed upon us in the busyness of life. We absolutely must set time aside to "go to our hiding place," which is like our spiritual Sabbath-time, to rebuild, restore and replenish our soul **(Isaiah 61:4)**. This is how we maintain balance and clear thinking. I call these breaks 'sanity times,' where we connect with God to fill up with His love and peace.

We function more effectively from a place of peace, than when we are caught up in the hectic pace of life. Again, our choice! A picture comes to mind of a light bulb connected to its source of power, emitting a bright light, versus a bulb loosely connected, where it emits a dim, sporadic light. As your faith increases by trusting God with all your heart, mind and strength **(Luke 10:27)**, your connectedness with God is also increased, so that you 'emit' more of His glory in your everyday life. In this place you become a lamp shining light into dark places.

The quality of your circumstances will also reflect this deeper connection with Him. Expand your vision for yourself by aligning with God.

DARE TO DREAM

Children are born to dream, imagine, explore, play, laugh and celebrate childhood, without hindrances or restrictions being placed upon them. Fear is not something they are born with. Babies are vessels open to be loved, cared for and have all their needs met without having to ask for anything. In their helpless state they instinctively 'expect' to be adored, cherished, loved unconditionally and nurtured. As they become toddlers, their sense of adventure increases; they 'push their boundaries' and, because they feel safe, their trust level has no limitation. Most of us lose our childlike qualities as we grow older. We are 'taught' and influenced by our parents, teachers and society to conform to their standards and beliefs, which have most likely been handed down from generation to generation. We have limitations and restrictions placed upon us, often causing us to fear the unknown.

How do we overcome learned mindsets?

- Firstly, we need to recognize we are not limited to what we have been taught.
- We CAN change our thoughts to form a new belief system, thus becoming what we were born to be (it is never too late for positive changes to occur)!
- Change is a process! As you choose to "think upon good things" (**Philippians 4:8**), realize your thoughts are profoundly affecting positive changes in your brain, and ultimately, your life. As you re-structure your thought life, you will attract new, more positive circumstances, opportunities and people to you, just as a magnet attracts another magnet to itself.
- As we realign our thoughts to come into agreement with who God created us to be, we are being restored to the "child within us," with unlimited potential to fulfill the dreams placed in us as young children. We "dare to dream" again! This process restores in us the ability to trust, to live confidently and move forward without

fears holding us back. Try to visualize how you felt as a young child, to recapture the essence of who you really are. Allow your imagination free rein to explore buried dreams and hopes within you, to fan the flame of life in your heart and soul, to re-awaken your childlike senses. **They have not died or been destroyed!** The essence of your true self is waiting to be stirred again by the renewal of your mind **(Romans 12:2).** You can be sure your soul (mind, will and emotions) will respond positively, to reflect the transformation that is taking place in your thoughts.

- Consciously visualize (see yourself) how your life will look when you are free from the old mindsets and limitations you believed about yourself. When old negative thoughts come to mind, realize they are separate from your true self, and are not a part of who you are becoming. Command them to "go" with authority and conviction. Choose to focus on what is good and worthwhile (your dreams and goals). To help you in this process, surround yourself with helpful books, inspiring sayings, and Scriptures that will uplift and encourage you. Listen to beautiful music, take walks in nature, meditate upon what God is speaking into your heart. Journal and seek wisdom in whatever circumstances you are dealing with, that threaten to overwhelm and frustrate you. As you make these changes in your lifestyle, you are 'feeding your inner being' with new life, thus 'starving' your old beliefs about yourself. Do not accept thoughts that threaten to hold you back from everything God has promised you. Make the following declaration over your life to reinforce the new life you have chosen.

"I CHOOSE GOD'S BEST FOR MYSELF AS I FOLLOW THE DREAMS HE PLACED IN ME AS A CHILD. I REJECT OLD LIES THAT HELD ME BACK IN THE PAST. I AM A CHILD OF GOD WHO LOVES ME AS I AM. I NOW STEP INTO ALL HIS PROMISES FOR ME, WITH THANKFULNESS IN MY HEART."

Ask yourself: What will my new life look like as I choose to follow God's Way?

Meditate on the following Declarations as you begin each new day:

- *I am "conformed into the image of God," with clarity of vision, meaning "my light bulb" is plugged into God's best for me.*

- *I am able to live fully in the "now" moment, where I can have peace as I face the challenges each day presents to me.*

- *I am able to see myself as an integral part of God's unfolding plans for my life, accepting the truth that "I have more than enough to meet my needs" (**Luke 12:25 - NIV**) **"Who of you by worrying can add a single hour to his life? Since you cannot do this very little thing, why do you worry about the rest?"***

- *I 'expect' to be blessed in my coming and going, whatever my circumstances may look like right now. I am not limited by foreboding thoughts and fears, because I know my life is changing for the better as I "think upon good things" (**Philippians 4:8**).*

- *As I take authority over my thought life, I will see positive changes occurring which will encourage me to continue on this new path.*

- *I choose to 'reclaim' old, buried dreams, which stirs new hope in my soul to reconnect with them. I believe once again in myself, to re-awaken these cherished dreams and make them real in my life.*

- *I have the wisdom to set healthy boundaries in my life, and the power to take a stand against anything that reduces the quality of my life.*

- *I have peace in my heart and clarity in my mind, as I move forward with confidence towards a good future, living each day with expectancy of God's best in my life.*

103

Secrets of the Hiding Place

I am not defined by my circumstances, unless I allow them to limit who I truly am.

Your heart is like a garden. Whatever you plant there will ultimately grow. Guard your heart at all times.

DARE TO DREAM

Dreams are elusive, secrets in our heart,
seeds of greatness awaiting God's touch
to bring them to life, stirring new hope
as we water them with our thoughts and our love.

Dreams die from neglect when we depart
from who we were as a little child.
We lose our way in complexity,
taking wrong turns away from our dreams.

God planted these dreams to be released
on our journey through life when we trust in Him.
The pathway is clear for us to see
as we open our eyes to our destiny.

Dare to dream, to imagine and seek
who you are and why you're here.
Stir yourself to follow Truth.
Follow your heart and choose to believe.

See yourself for who you are,
a child of God who was born to go far.
Follow the path He destined for you.
Wake up and become alive and renewed.

REFLECTIONS

- Describe what healthy boundaries are for you.

- Why do we need boundaries?

- Are there any unhealthy habits and mindsets you would like to eliminate from your life? Write them down, to give yourself a clear vision of what they are. Realize they can be overcome by your decisions to change your thoughts, as you choose God's kingdom values.

- What healthy boundaries would you like to establish to improve the quality of your life?

- How will you achieve this?

- How does "entering your Hiding Place with God" help you make positive changes in your life?

- Study the steps laid out in this chapter to help you in this process.

- Are you ready to follow your dreams, by making fundamental changes in what you believe about yourself?

- What will your life look like when you choose to follow your dreams? (Meditate upon the Declarations written at the end of this chapter as you begin each new day).

Chapter Seven

GOD'S BEST FOR US

Scripture: John 14:27 (ELB)

"Peace I leave with you. My own peace I now give and bequeath to you. Not as the world gives do I give to you. Do not let your hearts be troubled, neither let them be afraid. (Stop allowing yourselves to be agitated and disturbed, and do not permit yourselves to be fearful and intimidated and cowardly and unsettled)."

What is God's best for us?

God's best for us is higher than anything we can imagine this world can give us. If we were to receive everything we ask for; unlimited riches, ideal relationships, and perfect health, time would reveal that these things will not provide God's glorious riches from Heaven for us. What are these riches?

- God's unconditional love for us
- Peace that passes all understanding
- Inner contentment
- Wisdom to give us an eternal perspective
- Abiding thankfulness
- Strength to overcome adversity
- God's justice when we experience injustices against us
- Unconditional acceptance

As I have grown older, the greatest gift God has given me is the joy I experience in His presence. I actually hunger to be with Him **(Song of Songs 2:10 - LASB) "Rise up, my beloved, my fair one, and come away. For the winter is past, and the rain is over and gone."** The love I feel in my heart and soul gives me a deep sense of belonging, where I feel grounded (planted) in eternal values **(Isaiah 61:3).** It is in this place I have the awareness that I am exactly where I am supposed to be. I now understand that all my past experiences, no matter how painful, have led me to this point in time where my roots are planted in holy soil. Regardless of what the future may bring, I stand strong and firm in this place with God. It is in this place we receive all His blessings of love, peace, joy, fulfillment, wisdom, contentment, thankfulness, and hope for the future. The world cannot give us these gifts. From one day to the next, we never know what challenges we will encounter. Life runs smoothly for a while, then wham! Something unexpected throws us off balance on the roller coaster of our lives.

Secret of the Hiding Place

Thankfulness is like the morning dew in our heart, refreshing our soul.

What is God's will for us?

We are called to "prepare the Way" of the Lord by declaring His Truths with our thoughts and words. How do we conquer injustices and overcome evil? We *speak* what God would speak into our circumstances. We declare heavenly justice into our situations by taking a stand and confronting injustices, whatever form they may take. We do this by speaking out aloud chosen Scriptures dealing with whatever particular situation we are faced with. *There is power behind God's words that can be released into whatever we are going through.* To "prepare the way" for God to act on our behalf, we must take a stand for His Way and not bow down to fear. *This is how the River of Life from heaven is released onto earth.* We have access to this power when we become a mouthpiece of God's truths, to establish His kingdom values into our lives. As we trust God by standing on the Rock of His Word, He trusts us and pours His River of Life into our circumstances.

There is no earthly power greater than God. As we "come into agreement" with this truth, we become effective disciples to establish God's kingdom principles into our personal lives, and into the lives of whoever crosses our path. This is how we establish a Holy atmosphere for God to pour His will and promises *into* and *through* us.

What holds us back from receiving God's best for us?

- Do you have peace in your heart, even when facing disturbances around you?
- Do you negate yourself by speaking words that reflect a low self-esteem?
- Are you overly concerned about how you appear to others?
- Do you compare yourself to others, feeling inadequate when you don't 'measure up' to your own expectations?
- Do you often feel overwhelmed by your circumstances?
- Do you have a fatalistic outlook, believing nothing will change, regardless of what you do or how hard you try?
- Do you feel you always have to run to keep up with the demands in your life?
- Do you feel 'out of control,' confused and frustrated much of the time?
- Do you feel the need to apologize, even when something is not your fault?

Believing we are unworthy is a horrible way to live, for it leads to feeling victimized by circumstances, rather than being free to live as God would choose for us. When living under the burdens of fear, worry or anxiety, we are imprisoned by lies that limit us from receiving God's best. We cannot change our past, but we always have the choice to change how we think about the present, which leads to a more fulfilled future. As Scripture tells us: "Choose life instead of death" from this time onwards. In order to see ourselves as worthy of receiving a better life, we must make the decision to "ask for what we want" **(Matthew 7:7-8 - NIV) "Ask and it will be given to you; seek and you will find; knock and the door will be opened to you. For everyone who asks receives; he who seeks finds; and to him who knocks, the door will**

be opened." As we choose to agree with God's plan for our life, new opportunities for positive changes will be opened up. I wrote earlier about changing our mindset to conform to what God says about us. Here are some proclamations to read, meditate upon and declare out loud to reinforce positive transformations in your life.

PROCLAMATIONS TO DECLARE VERBALLY OVER YOUR LIFE

- **I am created in God's image, therefore, because of Jesus' sacrifice, I have been made worthy of receiving His unconditional love for me.**

- **I am not a mistake. I am a child of God, therefore I have legal access to inherit His promises for me.**

- **Feeling unworthy is a lie of the enemy. I choose to believe God's Word over all lies.**

- **I am a "work in progress" and I choose to trust God to lead, comfort and guide me on my life journey from this point forward.**

- **I choose to be patient with myself when I don't meet my own expectations.**

- **I do not need to strive in my own strength to bring about transformation.**

- **I am transformed by God's grace, as I choose to abide in His presence.**

- **I give all my burdens to Christ Jesus to carry for me (Matthew 11:30).**

- **My "hiding place in God" is where I go in my thoughts to find peace and solitude, regardless of whatever circumstances I may be dealing with.**

- **I am worthy of receiving God's best because He loves me as I am.**

Secrets of the Hiding Place

Happiness will always elude you if you chase after it.

When you have a "heart revelation" that you are completely loved by God, you are set free to be real and live your authentic life.

Another issue which can prevent us from stepping into the blessings of God, is the need to be in control of situations that would best be released to Him.

The need to be in control

- Are you uncomfortable when circumstances in your life are out of sync, when things do not go your way, when life throws you a 'curve-ball' that causes you to panic or feel frantic?
- Is your peace easily disturbed by 'unexpected' happenings, when you feel you are not prepared to cope with confusion?
- Do you feel frustrated when the people in your life do not conform to what you expect from them?
- Do you have anger issues when things do not go your way?
- Do you have a need to constantly make plans and daily lists in order to feel in control of what happens in your life?
- Do you experience fear, and a sense of being overwhelmed when your plans are unexpectedly disturbed?
- Is it very important to you to be right when anyone opposes your point of view?
- Do you react to opposing views with an argumentative attitude, frustration and impatience?
- Are you hard on yourself when you make mistakes?

- Do you experience bouts of depression and fatalistic thinking?

The problems listed above reveal mental thought patterns, stemming from negative self-beliefs that need to be changed. We can separate ourselves from our old beliefs when we really want to. This information should encourage rather than discourage you. Why? Because it reveals change is possible, according to the choices we make. We can all change from our old ways of thinking, by choosing to focus on new, life-giving thoughts that will ultimately create new beliefs, as well as positive emotions. As we do this, we 'switch on' new growth cells in our brain, causing healthy chemicals like serotonin to be released into our body (calming our nervous system). The need to be in control stems from being disconnected with your "true self" that was likely stolen from you as a child, possibly through some form of abuse; or perhaps a dysfunctional environment that caused you to experience physical or emotional pain. The abuse issues can be anything that left you feeling emotionally violated, unloved, abandoned, rejected, or being forced to grow up too quickly (by having to assume adult responsibilities too soon). When this occurs early in life, children are robbed of the emotional security they need to grow up feeling safe and protected. If you relate to any of these issues, believe with all your heart you can be restored to a healthy emotional state. The key is to recognize the problems you experienced, and be open to the help available to restore your true identity.

Please meditate upon the following Scriptures as often as possible to help you form new thought patterns and beliefs in your brain. I recommend you declare them verbally out loud on a regular basis, to help reinforce their positive effect in your life. These are wonderful, life-filled thoughts taken from the Bible to build you up, to restore your identity and what you believe about yourself.

SCRIPTURES TO MEDITATE UPON

Ephesians 3:20-21
"Now to Him who is able to do immeasurably more than all we ask or imagine, according to His power that is at work within us, to Him be glory in the church and in Christ Jesus throughout all generations."

Philippians 4:4-7
"Rejoice in the Lord always. Let your gentleness be evident to all. Do not be anxious about anything, but in everything, by prayer and petition, with thanksgiving, present your requests to God. And the peace of God, which transcends all understanding, will guard your hearts and your minds in Christ Jesus."

Psalm 34:18
"The Lord is close to the brokenhearted and saves those who are crushed in spirit."

Romans 8:28
"We know that in all things God works for the good of those who love Him, who have been called according to His purpose."

Matthew 17:20-21
"I tell you the truth, if you have faith as small as a mustard seed, you can say to this mountain, 'Move from here to there' and it will move. Nothing is impossible for you."

Matthew 4:4
"Man does not live on bread alone, but on every word that comes from the mouth of God."

Deuteronomy 31:6
"Be strong and courageous. Do not be afraid or terrified, for the Lord your God goes with you; He will never leave you nor forsake you."

Hebrews 11:1
"What is faith? It is the confident assurance that what we hope for is going to happen. It is the evidence of things we cannot yet see."

Proverbs 3:5-6
"Trust in the Lord with all your heart; do not depend on your own understanding. Seek His will in all you do, and He will direct your paths."

2 Corinthians 9:8
"God is able to make all grace abound to you, so that in all things at all times, having all that you need, you will abound in every good work."

Psalm 23:4
"Even though I walk through the valley of the shadow of death, I will fear no evil, for You are with me."

Psalm 27:1
"The Lord is my light and my salvation – whom shall I fear? The Lord is the stronghold of my life – of whom shall I be afraid?"

Psalm 27:4-5
"One thing I ask of the Lord, this is what I seek; that I may dwell in the house of the Lord all the days of my life, to gaze upon the beauty of the Lord, and to seek Him in His temple."

Psalm 27:13-14
"I am confident of this; I will see the goodness of the Lord in the land of the living. Wait for the Lord; be strong and take heart and wait for the Lord."

James 1:5-6
"If any of you lacks wisdom, he should ask God, who gives generously to all without finding fault, and it will be given to him. But when he asks, he must believe and not doubt."

Philippians 4:13
"I can do everything through Christ who gives me strength."

Matthew 11:28-30
"Come to me, all you who are weary and burdened, and I will give you rest. Take My yoke upon you and learn from Me, for I am gentle and humble in heart, and you will find rest for your souls. For My yoke is easy and My burden is light."

HOW DO WE ACHIEVE VICTORY IN OUR TRIALS?

Scripture: Isaiah 40:31 (NIV)

"Those who hope in the Lord will renew their strength. They will soar on wings like eagles; they will run and not grow weary; they will walk and not be faint."

Firstly, let us address why we experience trials. We all do, in our human condition. The nature and severity of our trials of course vary. Whenever I complain about whatever is challenging me, I have learned to be thankful as I observe the greater suffering of others around me, and in the world at large. I am left in awe by how much people suffer, yet continue to survive with a good attitude. Regarding the question of why people suffer, I do not have an answer that satisfies me, yet I do know God gives us the grace and strength to go through our valleys, when we ask Him for help. In my latter years, God has revealed to me some wisdom that has given me more understanding of the purpose and benefits of trials. When faced with conflict and challenges that threaten to steal your peace and equilibrium, the following are steps that will help you survive, and sometimes even to give thanks for the circumstances in your life.

- Realize that God is "good all the time" and will never leave nor harm you. **(Deuteronomy 31:8 - NIV) "The Lord Himself goes before you; He will never leave you nor forsake you. Do not be afraid. Do not be discouraged."**
- Ask God to reveal His divine purposes in this particular trial.
- Meditate on Scriptures pertinent to whatever you are going through.

Secret of the Hiding Place

The level of stress we experience from our circumstances is comparable to what we believe about these circumstances.

Scriptures to focus on during trials to align with God's truths

Feeling overwhelmed

Psalm 142:5-6 (NIV) "I cry to you O Lord. I say: You are my refuge, my portion in the land of the living. Listen to my cry, for I am in desperate need."

Psalm 62:1-2 (NLT) "I wait quietly before God, for my salvation comes from Him. He alone is my rock and my salvation, my fortress where I will never be shaken."

Needing comfort

Psalm 103:2-5 (NIV) "Praise the Lord O my soul, and forget not all His benefits, who forgives all your sins and heals all your diseases, who redeems your life from the pit and crowns you with love and compassion, who satisfies your desires with good things so that your youth is renewed like the eagle's."

Psalm 73:28 (NLT) "But as for me, how good it is to be near God! I have made the Sovereign Lord my shelter, and I will tell everyone about the wonderful things you do."

Feeling hopeless

Romans 15:13 (NIV) "May the God of hope fill you with all joy and peace as you trust in Him, so that you may overflow with hope by the power of the Holy Spirit."

1 Thessalonians 5:23-24 (NIV) "May God Himself, the God of peace, sanctify you through and through. May your whole spirit, soul and body be kept blameless at the coming of our Lord Jesus Christ. The One who calls you is faithful and He will do it."

Dealing with Grief

Isaiah 41:10 (NIV) "Do not fear, for I am with you; do not be dismayed, for I am your God. I will strengthen you and help you; I will uphold you with My right hand."

Revelation 21:4 (NIV) "He will wipe every tear from their eyes. There will be no more death or mourning or crying or pain, for the old order of things has passed away."

Feeling Fearful

Isaiah 43:1-3 (NIV) "Fear not, for I have redeemed you; I have summoned you by name; you are mine. When you pass through the waters, I will be with you. When you walk through the fire, you will not be burned."

Zephaniah 3:16-17 (NIV) "Do not fear, O Zion; do not let your hands hang limp. The Lord your God is with you, He is mighty to save. He will take great delight in you, He will quiet you with His love, He will rejoice over you with singing."

Feeling Anxious and Worried

Psalm 91:9-10 (NLT) "If you make the Lord your refuge, if you make the Most High your shelter, no evil will conquer you."

Psalm 23:1 (NLT) "The Lord is my Shepherd; I shall not want. He makes me to lie down in green pastures; He leads me beside the still waters; He restores my soul."

Feeling Lonely

Psalm 94:17-19 (NLT) "Unless the Lord had helped me, I would soon have died. I cried out 'I am slipping,' and Your unfailing love O Lord, supported me. When doubts filled my mind, Your comfort gave me renewed hope and cheer."

Lamentations 3:25-26 (NIV) "The Lord is good to those whose hope is in Him, to the one who seeks Him; it is good to wait quietly for the salvation of the Lord."

Feeling Desperate

Isaiah 51:11 (NIV) "The ransomed of the Lord will return. They will enter Zion with singing; everlasting joy will crown their heads. Gladness and joy will overtake them, and sorrow and sighing will flee away."

Psalm 91:14-16 (NLT) The Lord says, "I will rescue those who love me. I will protect those who trust in my name. When they call on me, I will answer. I will be with them in trouble. I will rescue them and honour them. I will satisfy them with a long life and give them my salvation."

Rejection and Abandonment

2 Timothy 4:16-17 (NIV) "At my first defense, no-one came to my support, but everyone deserted me. But the Lord stood at my side and gave me strength."

1 Peter 5:6-7 (NLT) "So humble yourselves under the almighty power of God, and in his good time he will honour you. Give all your worries and cares to God, for he cares about what happens to you."

Secret of the Hiding Place

Our darkest moments hold the promise of hope, new beginnings and healing as we press into God. His Light breaks through the clouds of hopelessness in our life, as rain and sunshine bring rainbows of promised blessings to us, when we turn our face towards Him.

Scripture: Romans 8:11 (NLT)

"The Spirit of God, who raised Jesus from the dead, lives in you. And just as He raised Christ from the dead, He will give life to your mortal body by this same Spirit living within you."

The more willing we are to 'lay down' our old ways of dealing with problems, the closer we draw in our heart to God, and the freedom He offers us. Freedom means living in His truths rather than confusion, chaos, doubt, worry, fear and frustration.

Exercise to simplify your life:

When faced with confusion about how to deal with daily challenges, ask yourself the following questions:

- What outcome do I want from this situation (whatever you are faced with)?
- How can I achieve the outcome I want?
- What will my life look like when I achieve this outcome?
- What changes must I make in my thoughts and actions to bring this about?

I suggest you journal your answers to the above questions, whenever you believe you need to change how you used to cope with stressful situations.

As long as we 'hold onto' our own issues, meaning we carry our burdens in our heart, mind and soul, we are seeing them through eyes that lack God's perspective. We are preventing the light of Truth from shining on our circumstances. We grope for answers in the darkness of our tormented emotions, falling into confusion, fear and anxiety that steal our peace. Can you relate to this scenario of how lost we feel by not releasing our cares to God? I certainly can. This is how I lived most of my life, in fear and uncertainty of the unknown. It was not until I "entered the rest of God" that I came to a place of peace. As I surrendered control of my life to Him, by choosing to trust God's ways over and above my own, I was then equipped to go through life's storms with confidence, knowing "He will never leave me nor forsake me" **(Deuteronomy 31:8).** In other words, I "made room for God" in my soul for Him to shine His Light and Wisdom into my circumstances. This is where transformation takes place! **(Romans 12:2 - NIV) "Do not conform any longer to the pattern of this world, but be transformed by the renewing of your mind."**

Please think about the choices you make as you deal with the challenges in your life! Ask yourself:

"Do I want to continue living as I have in the past?"

Or

"Do I want more peace and freedom in my mind and soul by choosing God's Way?"

In the process of making new choices, this will require a willingness to 'turn your ship' (your life) in a new direction. How do you do this? By consciously choosing to think new thoughts aligned with God's promises for you. As you take your focus off the circumstances you are going through, and re-focus on what God is revealing to you through the wisdom in His Words, your emotions will settle. This is how you enter peace during the storms of your life. This is how you overcome evil! Darkness cannot prevail in light, and you are an instrument of God's Light when you seek His presence in your circumstances. As you **believe** God is greater than anything you are being challenged by, you are choosing to connect with God's awesome power that overcomes ALL evil. You cannot lose when you partner with God!

Secret of the Hiding Place

We are only defeated when we believe we are!

God is waiting for us to surrender all our painful circumstances to Him completely.

This is how we 'make room' for Him to act on our behalf! We "create a place for God" by *stepping out of the way*. **Whatever pain you are holding onto, this part of you remains broken.** It is only as you surrender every hurt, trauma, unforgiveness, offense, self-pity, and all buried pain not dealt with to Jesus Christ, that you can "step into" the freedom God promises you. Give each broken piece of your heart and soul to Him, and He will restore you to wholeness.

Pray this prayer as you declare to God what you are willing to surrender, as you step into His will for your life.

PRAYER OF SURRENDER TO GOD

"**I give you my heart Lord; I give you my mind and my soul.**

I give every broken part of me to you Jesus.

I hold nothing back.

I belong to you – every broken piece of me belongs to you.

I surrender everything preventing me from loving you and receiving your love for me.

Take control of my life Lord.

Nothing else matters but you Lord.

Your justice is higher than man's injustices.

Lord, fill these hands so that I may give as you give.

Fill my heart with your amazing grace, your abiding peace, your everlasting love.

Make me a blessing in your sight.

Guide me with your Truth and make me a vessel of your love." Amen.

Secret of the Hiding Place

Whatever circumstances you may be experiencing, seek God and you will find Him. It is in this place with God that we are transformed into His likeness, to overcome all adversity.

REFLECTIONS

- What do you believe is God's best for you?

- Describe what you think may be preventing you from receiving God's best in your life. (Refer to questions in this chapter pertaining to this question).

- Meditate on the Scriptures quoted in this chapter to help you understand God's will for you.

- How do we achieve victory in our trials? (Refer to Scriptures quoted to help you in specific challenges you are faced with).

- Do the exercise in this chapter to simplify your life. Journal the questions asked and reflect on what God reveals to you through these questions.

- Pray the Prayer of Surrender to help you align with God's will for you.

Chapter Eight

ESTABLISHING HEALTHY PRIORITIES

*I*n our world of high-tech communication, we can access information instantly from anywhere across our globe. This technological breakthrough was originally supposed to simplify our lives. Computers have opened up limitless resources for us to tap into with a flick on our icon. We have the world at our fingertips, and that is an awesome phenomenon our ancestors could not have imagined in past eras. Picture your grandparents returning momentarily to this new Age we live in, endeavouring to adapt to what we now take for granted. My grandparents' transportation was a horse and buggy, which they used for delivering paper bags they manufactured at the factory in their backyard. Their customers were merchants selling their wares in open markets. They heated up bricks to place their feet on in the open horse-drawn buggy, and wrapped themselves in blankets to travel to various markets at 4 am each morning. A letter written by hand to someone overseas took many weeks to arrive. They created their own entertainment by having musical evenings in their home; Grandpa was a concert pianist and Nana an opera singer. As I was growing up, my Nana took me to musical concerts performed at the Melbourne Botanical Gardens, where we sat on a blanket laid out on the grass in this informal atmosphere. This is how I was introduced to opera at an early age. I share these memories to reveal some of the priorities and values of past generations. They were not exposed to the 'overload' of information from across the world as we are, moment by moment into our daily lives. I believe we have lost something precious, that is, the time and opportunity to reflect and meditate upon what we are exposed to. We have lost the art of simplicity, meaning life and information is moving at such a frantic pace, we get caught up in racing through each day to get to the next day, and the next day, as quickly as possible. We rarely take time to think about the importance of reflecting upon each 'now' moment.

How can we hear what God is communicating to us when we rarely stop to 'listen' to our inner voice, which is Holy Spirit living in us? How can we access our "hiding place" where hidden treasures of truth await discovery by us, if only we would take the time to listen? How can we separate our important priorities from the busyness of life, when we don't meditate on them? It is comparable to constantly eating food that needs to be digested before we eat our next meal. How do we discover our uniqueness and inner gifts, when we don't prioritize and separate ourselves long enough to make healthy, life-giving choices about discovering who we really are, and where our lifestyle is taking us? We need more "Sabbath" rests in our busy schedules to establish what is really important to us. We need to set aside time from our addiction to constant communication on our iphones and ipads, to connect with our "inner-self." This is the "hidden place" that we can plug into in our deeper consciousness. This is where our heart is waiting to be heard!

What is your heart saying to you?

Secrets of the Hiding Place

Simplicity is choosing what is right for you.

Do not give too much importance to unimportant things.

Your heart beliefs are the blueprint of what you really believe and how you see yourself. Your identity is rooted in your heart. What you believe about yourself stems from what you were taught while growing up, what people close to you spoke into your mind, and how you were treated as a child. As you grew older, your values were formed by the world around you, as you were exposed to information in your physical environment. Here are some questions you may wish to ask yourself to help you identity what you believe in your heart.

- What priorities became important to you as a child?
- Were you loved, guided and protected as you grew up?
- Did you feel safe as you explored the world around you?
- Did you mature with a sense of self-worth, with inner security and confidence to move beyond the protective boundaries set by others?

If you were raised in such an environment, you were truly blessed. Many of us were not as fortunate, therefore our heart beliefs about ourselves require a new set of beliefs, in order to transform who we believe ourselves to be.

There is Hope!

Establishing a new set of beliefs is not an impossible task! The first step is to realize you *can* change if you *want* to.

The second step is to journal what needs to be changed.

Write out in detail what you believe about yourself. Look at how you were raised and how you perceived yourself as a young child, which is when your identity was formed.

- How did you relate to other children, your parents, and your teachers?
- Were you confident or shy, a leader or a follower?
- Did you have self-confidence, or did you experience many fears?
- Were you adventurous or cautious?
- Was it overly important to you to please others and be affirmed, or were you a self-starter who boldly stepped beyond others' expectations of you?

124

These and other questions can reveal the "inner you," the positive and negative beliefs that formed the foundation of who you are now. This helps you to recognize what changes could benefit and help you to establish new beliefs about yourself, and what you would like to incorporate into how you want to live. As explained earlier, this is entirely possible through choosing new thought patterns that ultimately form new heart beliefs.

The next step is to journal what changes you would like to make in your life. Do not limit your expectations about yourself, based on how you lived in the past.

Scriptures: Luke 18:27 (NIV) "What is impossible with men is possible with God."

Philippians 4:13 (NIV) "I can do all things through Christ who gives me strength."

Be specific and detailed in what you would like to change, what you see for yourself, and what this would look like in your life. This may apply to your intimate relationships, your career, dreams you would like to pursue, financial goals, hidden desires of your heart; (perhaps what you aspired to do as a child). The sky is the limit, for you have unlimited potential to tap into.

When you have done this, prioritize what is most important to you, then consciously decide to "come into agreement in your thoughts" with these dreams you hold in your heart. This means you become a "watchman over your thoughts." If you notice thoughts of fear, doubt or unbelief entering your mind, speak out loud (verbalize) words against them (**2 Timothy 1:7 - NIV) "For God does not give us a spirit of timidity, but a spirit of power, of love and of self-discipline."** Be committed to this process, knowing God lives in you. **"Everything is possible to those who believe" (Mark 9:23).**

The wonder of your life is only limited by your perception of it!

As you re-train your brain with positive, belief-filled thoughts, your emotions will respond, so that ultimately you will become what you believe yourself to be. Declare out loud to yourself:

"I am only limited by my own beliefs and who I see myself to be. I choose to believe what God says about me." (Quote the above Scriptures verbally and claim them for yourself personally).

Your feelings stem from what you believe in your heart, which can be likened to your sub-conscious mind. You instinctively react from your heart memories, those impressions stamped upon your heart in childhood. I see those memories as someone "walking on your heart, leaving their footprints behind." These footprints have created a pattern of beliefs, forming our identity while we were young. A child is like a moldable piece of clay that can be shaped by outside influences, good and bad. Their emotions are open, trusting others without question; they believe what they are taught, because they have not yet developed defenses to protect themselves. They are uncomplicated and honest, responding to love or abuse by taking on the belief they must deserve what is happening to them. In other words, the foundation of who they believe themselves to be has been laid (stamped in their heart). When the foundations are positive, they grow into adults with a strong sense of self-worth, where they flourish and prosper in their life, just as a building constructed on a sound, stable foundation will stand strong and endure for a long time. When a child's foundations are built on abuse, shame, guilt or trauma of any kind, they take on these characteristics in their heart, and so believe this is who they are as they mature. Their foundational beliefs are 'off-kilter,' resulting in a poor self-image, with all the negative consequences attached to a low self-esteem.

Secret of the Hiding Place

Don't see yourself from the reflection of people's eyes; see yourself as a reflection of God's love.

We Can Change!

I write about these issues because I understand and know from my own experience that we do not have to remain prisoners of our past.

*The greatest motivator to change is the **desire** to change!*

Our brains are structured for change, just as the cells in our body are continually forming new cells as the old ones die. Our brain is renewed by our thoughts, which form our beliefs. We are created by God to be renewed every day. Study the words in the following Scripture from the Everyday Life Bible that explains what is truly meant by the renewal of your mind. I included this Scripture in an earlier chapter, however, this particular interpretation relates very well to what I am endeavouring to convey to you.

Scripture: Romans 12:2 (ELB)

"Do not be conformed to this world (this age), (fashioned after and adapted to its external, superficial customs), but be transformed (changed) by the (entire) renewal of your mind (by its new ideals and its new attitude), so that you may prove (for yourselves) what is the good and acceptable and perfect will of God, even the thing which is good and acceptable and perfect (in His sight for you)."

We are products of the continual cycle of renewal!

We are not immoveable objects, as though formed in cement. Every new day is an opportunity for us to make positive changes, by the renewal of our mind (our thoughts).

What prevents us from making positive changes?

We may know we need to change, but are not yet ready to commit to this process.

What do we need to do to motivate us to make changes in our life?

We need to **want** to change so much, we are prepared to give up our old ways of thinking and behaving to make this happen. **The power to change lies within us!** Once we recognize that the answers for everything we need to change live within us, this gives us hope to believe for a better life for ourselves. Some of us hold ourselves back because we have bought into the belief we are victims of our circumstances, which prevents us from moving forward towards positive change. We are not yet ready to 'throw off the cloak,' the invisible garment of believing we are a victim, because this is all we know. We automatically function and respond to who we believe we are, and are not yet ready to be accountable (meaning we are not willing to change), by 'throwing off' the old garment (our old identity). Why? Because we fear feeling vulnerable, of being 'uncovered,' as the cocoon of our old self has to be stripped away before we can emerge, to be who God created us to be. *The price for freedom is to turn away from old beliefs.*

DYING TO LIVE

Scripture: Galatians 2:20 (NLT)

"I myself no longer live, but Christ lives in me. So I live my life in this earthly body by trusting in the Son of God, who loved me and gave Himself for me."

I wrote in Chapter Two about the need for a seed to lose its shell (outer casing) before it can take root in the soil it is planted in. Scripture often refers to our need to "die to our flesh" before we can be transformed by the Spirit of God into His likeness. What does it really mean to die to our flesh? We may wonder why life is so difficult as we experience the pain of trials and losses, even as we 'press in' to do what we believe is right in our Christian journey. In seeking to understand God's perspective during seasons of suffering, I have studied Scriptures relating to what takes place within us during trials, which have brought me some revelation to share with you.

Dying to our flesh is a painful process. We are like children who need to be disciplined before we mature to adulthood. Discipline requires us to control our emotions, rather than allow them to rule us.

This does not occur naturally. Our emotions need to be harnessed (as a bridle on a horse) to direct them, under the control of our mind. If they are not under control, they manifest as pride, selfishness, willfulness, stubbornness, over-indulgence, anger, impatience, unforgiveness, and other negative qualities. We tend to have blinkers over our eyes when it comes to observing our own shortfalls. Often, it takes some calamity to reveal both our greatest strengths and weaknesses. It is usually when we are 'under pressure' from unpleasant circumstances, that our hidden qualities are brought to the surface, to show us what we need to learn. *Facing truth is both painful and freeing.* The more willing we are to seek truth, to align ourselves with what God is revealing to us, the closer we draw to Him. We need to be willing to 'let go' of our old defense strategies that protect our ego-self (our pride). As we stop trying to defend ourselves by justifying our old ways of handling stress, we enter into freedom. That is, the freedom to be real, authentic and vulnerable, without fear of being misunderstood by others. *Humility reveals strength in our character; it is not a weakness.*

Dying to ourselves does not mean we cannot enjoy the blessings of the world we live in. What it does mean is that we should not be controlled by our longings for these things. True freedom is the freedom from *needing* what the world offers us, where we can be happy and content with or without these things.

The shell of our fleshly self prevents us from taking root in God!

Blessings from choosing a lifestyle of following God:

- As our outer veneer (our old self) fades, we become like diamonds with many facets, where true beauty is revealed.
- We lose our fears of how we appear to others.
- We can be honest and effective in helping people as we share our heart, with motives aligned to God's heart.
- We connect with the power of God as we 'die' to all pretentiousness.
- We experience God's consuming peace, where life's trials do not disturb our feelings in a negative way.

- We become strong and stable, a force for good, to help others through their trials.
- We are able to speak God's wisdom into people's lives.

In other words, we 'die' to our old self and come alive to God's world of Truth. This is how we fulfill our earthly role, by becoming who God created us to be during our human journey. This is true freedom! The seed of God in us, His Holy Spirit, invades our soul, so that we become a reflection of His love, wisdom, peace and light. This is how we enter into the presence of God.

Scripture: John 12:24 (NLT)

"The truth is, a kernel of wheat must be planted in the soil. Unless it dies it will be alone – a single seed. But its death will produce many new kernels – a plentiful harvest of new lives."

The Process of Throwing Off Our Old Identity

As mentioned earlier, we have to want to change so much, we are prepared to take the risk of letting our 'old self' die. Going through this process causes us to feel undressed (exposed), where we may fear being open to new ways of thinking. As we choose to live by a new belief system (who God says we are), we enter into His world of limitless possibilities.

Change is a process!

Changing our old thought patterns and beliefs takes time. If we are not sincerely committed to this process, we will falter and 'fall back' to our old ways, thus becoming discouraged with ourselves.

What does commitment involve?

- Commitment is the determination to "stay the course" and never give up, regardless of how we may feel, even when we don't seem to be making progress.

- Commitment establishes 'guideposts' for us to follow, so that we do not stray and take our attention away from our goals.
- Commitment is a decision, deep within our heart, to focus on the goal we have set for ourselves; choosing to not allow the physical evidence (circumstances) presently existing in our life, to distract or discourage us.
- We "set our mind" on the goal ahead; we use our imagination to form a mental picture of where we are going. We visualize how we will feel (the emotions we will experience) once we reach our goal.

We live in this new reality for ourselves in our thoughts and feelings, as though we have already arrived there physically. We believe for "things that are not, as though they are" **(Romans 4:17).** What we are actually doing is forming the new reality of what we are 'choosing' to believe about ourselves. We are less influenced by our present physical circumstances than we may believe. Again, it takes a committed decision on our part to "stay the course," regardless of the obstacles we encounter. Think of the story of Alice in Wonderland by Lewis Carroll (see notes at end of book), where all the frightening experiences and strange creatures she encountered were really illusions of her mind. They had no real substance to them! Alice's fears were unfounded, because these illusions had no control over her. The same principle applies to us. Our fears are 'illusions' the enemy would have us believe. We have the choice to believe them, or not! Whatever we focus on becomes bigger and grows, as long as we are 'feeding' it through the thoughts we are choosing to think. Back to Alice, as she 'looked' at the creatures she encountered, they became bigger before her eyes. See your thoughts as creatures. Do you want them to increase and grow more important to you? If your answer is "no," stop thinking about them! *You have been given free will by God to choose what you want to think about.*

Once you make your decision to choose another way of thinking, commit yourself to "search with all your heart, mind and soul" **(Jeremiah 29:13),** and pursue the dreams God implanted in you before you were even born. As you do this, you are aligning yourself with whom God created you to be, a person with unlimited potential, to *"rise up and step beyond all the limiting boundaries and restrictions put upon you from your past."*

Secrets of the Hiding Place

My value is not in what I do, but in who I am in Christ Jesus.

Never give up on yourself. God hasn't!!!

It is so liberating to know you have access to the power of transformation in yourself, according to what you believe in your heart. The power within you is the same power Jesus Christ had access to when He lived on earth, the power of His Father in Heaven. Jesus knew who He was and listened to His Father at all times. He never acted on His own behalf. He always consulted His Father before He acted, for He knew He needed this connection to fulfill His destiny as the Son of God. Think about the significance of this amazing truth. **God lives in you!** When the power of God's Holy Spirit entered your body through asking Christ into your heart, you became a "home" to God, or in other words, a vessel for His presence to reside within you. You are literally 'plugged in' to the Kingdom of God, with access to His unlimited power and all His promises for you.

How do we live in the reality of what Jesus accomplished for us by His death, resurrection and ascension to the throne of God in Heaven?

Picture yourself with Jesus as He died on the cross, being with Him as He descended into darkness. He took all our sin with Him, meaning, our old identity has been buried and left behind (removed from us), now and forevermore. When Jesus ascended from darkness into Light as He was resurrected, picture yourself rising with Him into Heaven, to sit with Him at the right hand of God. This means you now have access to everything God offers to Jesus, His Son.

The only blocks preventing us from accessing God's power are our limited beliefs!

Scripture: Romans 8:35-39 (ESV)

"Who shall separate us from the love of Christ? Shall tribulation, or distress, or persecution, or danger, or sword? No, in all these things we are more than conquerors through Him who loves us. For I am sure that neither death nor life, nor angels nor rulers, nor things present nor things to come, will be able to separate us from the love of God in Christ Jesus our Lord."

Secrets of the Hiding Place

Celebrate who you are by recognizing "God moments" in your everyday life.

Although happiness may seem to elude us, the value of what we have in this "present moment" can be enough for us as we rest in God.

God loves you!

Do you believe this? Do you believe God is good all the time? **(Psalm 100:5 - NLT) "For the Lord is good. His unfailing love continues forever, and His faithfulness continues to each generation."** Can you accept that He wants you to be blessed with all the wonderful promises in Scripture? If we have doubts about whether God will respond to our prayers, this means we do not fully comprehend the all-encompassing love He has for us **(Ephesians 3:17 – NLT) "May your roots go down deep into the soil of God's most marvelous love."** Picture yourself as a little child sitting on Papa God's knees. He is delighting Himself in your presence, adoring you with His deep love as you snuggle into His protective arms. In this place you are safe, cherished, beloved, secure and fearless, because you know you will never be abandoned nor rejected by Father God. Can you see yourself being loved in this way? Can you receive His love right now? Are you able to allow yourself to abandon any negative views that have blocked you from feeling worthy of receiving God's love in the past? God does not see your flaws. He sees the beauty in your heart and soul. He sees what He created, and "it is good." As you see yourself in this way, you are open to being blessed as His child, which will transform your self-image.

When we give all of ourselves to Christ, He becomes everything to us!

Scripture: 1 Corinthians 15:28 (NLT)

"Then, when He has conquered all things, the Son will present Himself to God, so that God, who gave His Son authority over all things, will be utterly supreme over everything everywhere."

Jesus represents (stands in for us) to present us to God. This means we have an advocate to make all our needs and requests known to God our Father. When we pray in Jesus' name, we activate this godly principle in our personal lives. This is how we spiritually enter into the throne room of God. This is how God's justice is activated for us, when we call to Jesus for help. This is how we enter into God's presence. This is how miracles happen. As you believe how God sees you, you are open to being blessed as His child. This will enable you to feel worthy of receiving all the wonderful things God has promised. **Will you allow Him to lavish His love and blessings upon you?** Can you believe you were chosen for a purpose, that you are one of a kind, a pearl of great price, and worthy of God's best for you?

Secrets of the Hiding Place

Lasting joy is only limited by our limited expectations.

Your faith is the doorway that enables you to enter into the realm of God's limitless possibilities.

Boundaries and Their Lines of Demarcation

Scripture: Hebrews 4:12-13 (NIV)

"For the Word of God is living and active. Sharper than any double-edged sword, it penetrates even to dividing soul and spirit, joints and marrow; it judges the thoughts and attitudes of the heart. Nothing in all creation is hidden from God's sight. Everything is uncovered and laid bare before the eyes of Him to whom we must give account."

While I was in prayer and worshiping God, a picture formed in my mind, unfolding like a movie playing before my eyes. It was vivid, filled with clarity and meaning.

Vision

I saw dark, rolling storm clouds hovering over Earth. They appeared threatening, filled with thunder and lightning. As heavy rain poured down, the raindrops appeared to look like millions of white doves. Their wings were pressed close to their bodies, taking on the shape of teardrops. As the doves landed upon people whose eyes were focused towards the sky, their wings burst open to cover each person with God's anointed promises as they fluttered over them.

Interpretation

The storm clouds in our life are not there to bring destruction to us. They represent the tumultuous circumstances we are dealing with, where fears are stirred in us as we face overwhelming challenges. However, as long as we "look up" to God with trust in our heart, the dark clouds hold His promises to bless us through our pain. The doves represent God's Holy Spirit being poured out upon us, as we remain in position to receive His Holy Rain (Living Waters) from Heaven. The doves appearing in the shape of teardrops represent God's tears for us when we suffer. As we focus wholly upon God, seeking His presence first, over and above all of our circumstances, the doves open their wings to bless us with His anointed power poured out upon us (protecting us from all harm, regardless of the 'terrors of night' threatening us). The doves bring promises of breakthroughs in whatever storms we are facing. As we take our stand, by holding our position in God's kingdom values, victory and good outcomes are assured, whatever our circumstances may look like in the natural world.

We can make new choices!

God loves ALL people! It is the spirit of deception and lies that causes people to make wrong choices. We have been given free will to choose "life or death" (**Deuteronomy 30:19**) during our short lifespan. The responsibility lies with each one of us to make our own choices. What does it mean to "choose life?"

Choosing life means:

- Forgiving those who hurt us.
- Forgiving ourselves for unwise choices in our past.
- Choosing to resist taking offenses from others' words and actions towards us. (Allowing the spirit of offense into our heart can wound us emotionally and physically).
- Obeying God and laying down the burdens Jesus died to remove from us.
- Choosing God's rest and peace, especially during the storms we encounter in our life.

We need to do our part by making right choices for ourselves!

We do this by surrendering our will (our mind, heart and emotions) to God's will (His kingdom values, which are the government of Heaven, as in the Lord's prayer) **Matthew 6:9-13 "Thy kingdom come, Thy will be done on Earth as it is in Heaven."**

Who or what rules your heart?

This is a question I ask myself when I want something so badly, I feel I cannot be happy until I receive whatever I am asking for.

Ask yourself: Whom do I "bow down to" in my choices?

Your own needs and desires?

Or

God and His eternal values?

From my own experiences in the past, I learned that I felt confident as long as life was going well. However, whenever I 'hit the wall' of circumstances that overwhelmed me, resulting in fear, my confidence in 'me' was shattered. I fell apart when the storms of life destroyed hope, and challenged all the strategies I had used in the past to survive.

God is waiting for us to choose His Way over the ways of the world!

Why should we choose His Way?

God created us to seek Him, to trust Him and have relationship with Him, the way a child naturally trusts its earthly father. God wants relationship with us, not out of duty, but because we are drawn to Him by love. Father God IS love and will never manipulate us to choose Him by force.

Scripture: Jeremiah 29:13 (NIV)

"You will seek Me and find Me when you seek Me with all your heart."

The rewards in choosing God's Way over our own desires are many:

- Peace beyond our human understanding.

- Communion with God in our spirit (the marriage of His eternal Spirit with our inner spirit).

- Wisdom and guidance to lead us through our valleys towards victory (meaning we overcome life's challenges and grow stronger through our trials).

- We dwell in the atmosphere of Heaven while going through difficult times.

- God communicates His eternal perspective through His Holy Spirit within us, giving us "eyes to see" the hidden purposes of our trials.

- We are never alone, ever again, for God is with us always.

- We live above the spirit of fear, therefore we are free in our heart to grow, and move forward towards our God-given destiny.

- We become a "new creature" (as a butterfly released from its cocoon).

- We experience joy amidst the chaos of our surroundings.

Secrets of the Hiding Place

Fear is a tool in the hands of our enemy, to bring us under the dominion of darkness.

Earth is a mirrored reflection of God's heavenly universe, waiting for mankind to recognize this truth.

REFLECTIONS

- Are you willing to change old habits in order to establish new boundaries, that lead to a more fulfilling life?

- How do we establish new beliefs in our life? (Follow the steps laid out in this chapter).

- What can you do personally to establish new beliefs and make them a reality in your life?

- What may be preventing you from making these changes? Be specific!

- Are you willing to let go of these blocks and move forward with God?

- Do you agree that simplicity is achieved by choosing what is right for you?

- What can you do to simplify your life?

- What does "dying to live" mean to you personally? (Galatians 2:20) "I myself no longer live, but Christ lives in me."

- Describe what it means to "throw off our old identity?"

- Do you believe in your heart that God loves you just as you are?

- If you have any doubts about this, think about how much you love your children or anyone very close to you, then transfer that love to yourself, to help you understand how much God loves you.

- How do we know what choices are good for us?

- Make a list of some of the benefits of choosing God's Way in the choices you make.

Chapter Nine

THE LORD'S PRAYER

Scripture: Matthew 6:9-13 (King James)

> **"Our Father who art in heaven,**
> **hallowed be thy name,**
> **Thy kingdom come, thy will be done**
> **in earth as it is in heaven.**
> **Give us this day, our daily bread,**
> **forgive us our trespasses,**
> **as we forgive those who trespass against us.**
> **And lead us not into temptation,**
> **but deliver us from evil;**
> **for thine is the kingdom, and the power, and the glory,**
> **for ever and ever,"**

Amen.

*T*he Lord's Prayer is God's blueprint for how we should live our lives. I suspect that if we truly understood what God is saying to us through this prayer, we would choose to live close to His heart and be blessed with everything He has for us on earth. Let us look at each phrase of Jesus' words in this prayer.

OUR FATHER WHO ART IN HEAVEN, HALLOWED BE THY NAME

In speaking these words, we are declaring who we believe God is, by honouring His name and what He represents to us. There are many names for God, each one revealing variations of His divine qualities and nature. As we acknowledge who God is in our prayers, we are connecting to His heart and all that He is to us. In Scripture, much is written about the power of God and His great love for us. When we declare with our words who God is and what he means to us personally, we are building relationship with Him for all eternity. Our life journey is very short, so it is extremely important to fill the time we have upon earth with every opportunity to know God better, to draw close to who He is by seeking to understand His character and His love for us. Here are some of the names to describe Christ Jesus. In the Hebrew language, Jesus is called Yeshua, which means He is our Salvation, our Deliverer and our Rescuer.

* Jehovah-Rophe	The Lord is our Healer	Exodus 15:26
* Jehovah-Shammah	The Lord is Present	Ezekiel 48:35
* Jehovah-Shalom	The Lord is our Peace	Judges 6:24
* Jehovah-Mikaddesh Kem	The Lord Sanctifies us	Exodus 31:13
* Jehovah-Tsidkenu	The Lord is our Righteousness	Jeremiah 23:6
* Jehovah-Jireh	The Lord is our Provider	Genesis 22:14

When we think highly of someone close to us, we want to know everything about them, so that we can build an intimate relationship with them. This truth also applies to drawing near to God as we pray to Him and seek His presence. The more we know about our Lord, the closer we draw to His heart and to His will in our lives.

Jehovah-Rophe – The Lord is our Healer – Exodus 15:26

I wrote extensively in The Cherished Piece about how God healed my brokenness from the past. This book was written as a testimony of how God healed my crushed emotions caused by sexual abuse as a child. Obviously this was an extremely painful season of my life, yet there is much good that has come from going through such trauma. God has restored my damaged emotions and given me back my life, so that now I am able to share how God is able to do **"exceedingly and abundantly, above and beyond anything we can imagine" (Ephesians 3:20)** to heal us, whatever our needs may be. I am living proof of this truth. The nature of God is to heal our brokenness and pain by His grace and great love for us. Be encouraged that He will heal you in every area of your life as you declare: *"Lord, You are my Healer, and I trust you as I believe, by faith, that You are with me always in my journey towards healing."*

Jehovah-Shammah – The Lord is Present – Ezekiel 48:35

How do *you* experience the presence of God? Do you sense He is with you, or does He seem distant and unapproachable? This is how I used to see God, before I understood He is present *in* me and *with* me every moment of my life. I wrote earlier about a man called Brother Lawrence, who lived in the 1600's as a monk in a monastery. His letters moved my heart profoundly, as he explained how he experienced the presence of God and what that meant to him. He was filled with the joy of God's Holy Spirit within him, causing him to live in a continual state of gratitude and thankfulness in his heart. He was constantly filled with God's great love for him. He was a humble man without attributes the world would consider valuable, yet he was "captured by God's love" to such an extent, he became a source of kindness, wisdom and compassion for others. His letters were written to people who sought his help at that time, and have been published in a small book called The Practice Of The Presence Of God for people to read hundreds of years after his death (see notes at end of book). *This love from God is available for all who seek to know who He is, and choose to believe and trust His Word.*

The presence of God is more real than anything we observe with our physical senses. Choose to trust Him, and be willing to wait for Him to move on your behalf.

Jehovah-Shalom – The Lord is our Peace – Judges 6:24

Abiding peace from God is a jewel of great price, not easily achieved, for it costs us the sacrifice of our own ego before we are able to live in contentment, and in the "rest" of God **(Psalm 23)**. When we make the choice to live in God's peace, this is where we hear the quiet, gentle voice of God's Holy Spirit leading us in the paths of Righteousness and Truth. It is in this place we experience God's presence and peace, where we are restored to wholeness, whatever our circumstances may be. We all lose our way and make poor decisions at times, yet God is ever-faithful to pick us up and comfort us, giving us hope for a new day as we rely on Him to be our guide.

Secrets of the Hiding Place

Our greatest error is not all the mistakes we make. It is our mistaken belief God will not use whatever happens to us for His ultimate good in our life.

Increase your expectations to align with God's promises to "heal, bless, protect, comfort, and provide for you."

Jehovah-Mikaddesh Kem – The Lord Sanctifies us – Exodus 31:13

To sanctify someone means they are set apart for a special purpose. This is a process of refinement, where anything that separates them from becoming sanctified has to be 'burned off' before they can be used for a special purpose. Think of how gold is liquefied, so that any impurities within it are removed through heat (which separates the gold from any dross), thus making it highly valuable. We cannot sanctify ourselves by our own efforts. God sees us as He created us, without any imperfections. *Our role is to surrender to the process of whatever God is doing through our circumstances, so that His greater purposes for us can be fulfilled in our lifetime.* God is changeless in our ever-changing world. As we learn to trust His greater good working through the pain we experience in our humanness, we change and become conformed to His image. It is in this place we can live with thankfulness in our heart for whatever we are going through, knowing we are drawing closer to God's heart, as we allow Him to refine and sanctify us for His purposes.

Qualities required to be conformed to God's sanctification process:

- Faithfulness
- Covenant with God's values
- Courage and boldness to take risks
- Conviction to stay the course, whatever opposes us
- Commitment
- Humility

The process of sanctification is gradual as we allow God to refine us, one step at a time, until we become a "mirror-image" of Christ. What does it take for us to be sanctified by God?

- An open heart inclined towards Him.
- Awareness that this life is the training ground for an eternal, God-given purpose for us.
- The realization that whatever we have to suffer and sacrifice is of little importance, compared to the life God has destined for us, not only here on earth, but in our eternal life in heaven.
- A hunger for the presence of God over and above whatever the world has to offer us.
- A willingness to allow God to have His Way with us as we rest and abide in His Shalom peace.
- The choice to be led by *love* rather than our own issues.
- An awareness that we have been given the gift of life for a greater purpose than pleasing ourselves, and following our own desires and doctrines.

Recently in prayer, God gave me a picture of what a sanctified life looks like. I would like to share this with you to help you understand what it means to come into God's will in your life.

We are alabaster vessels being broken by life's circumstances, as we die to those things that are familiar to us. These familiar things represent false walls of security and safety, preventing us from stepping into all God wants to give us. In the Bible, alabaster vessels contained perfume, which was considered highly valuable in ancient times. God is calling us to be willing to be broken to ourselves, so that the essence of our true selves can be poured out upon Him, meaning, to place God first by honouring who He is to us. This is the only way we can become a sweet perfume to God, when all worldly values and false protections are broken off from us.

Sanctification doesn't happen without us coming into agreement with this process. We "choose" to allow ourselves to be sanctified for a "greater purpose" as we surrender to God's will for us. What does this mean and how do we become sanctified? We either live for ourselves by settling for the shallow existence and values this entails, or, we commit our hearts and lives to what Christ Jesus sacrificed for us on the cross. As we experience painful trials, we choose to look at the bigger picture of what happens to us through the suffering we endure, rather than 'running away' from facing truth. How is your character formed? As you endure hardships, you discover what you are capable of, as hidden strengths rise up from within you to meet the challenges you face. As you meet these challenges in a godly way, you are being "sanctified" in the refining fire of life. Your character is being strengthened to promote you to a higher level of understanding, and a deepening of love and compassion in your heart for others. You become rich in the godly attributes of mercy, kindness, patience, peace and understanding as you become a "servant for God's divine purposes" to bless others. As you do this, you will also be blessed in ways you cannot imagine.

The Process of Transformation

In order to understand what transformation looks like in our life, we first need to know what takes place when we make the decision to accept Jesus Christ into our heart. The seed of God contains ALL that He is. His Holiness is implanted into us, and the process of transformation begins its cycle in our spirit, just as the seed of a flower ultimately develops into a beautiful creation. This is called a re-birth, being "born again" as our spirit unites with God's Holy Spirit. We cannot be transformed into Jesus' likeness until we are willing to be broken to our old self, the person Scripture calls the 'old man.' This entails our willingness to change, to repent for our previous beliefs and mindsets that defined who we were before God came to live in us. We need to 'lay down' these old ways of thinking at the cross, to make room for Holy Spirit to increase in our spirit. God cannot move into a house filled with old furniture (our old beliefs). As we open our heart to allow Holy Spirit to expand in us by believing His truths, transformation takes place within us. The 'veils of deception' fall away to reveal the Light of God in our soul, as we surrender to the process of 'dying to our old self.' This is how we choose Life instead of death for ourselves. We set into motion the process of transformation by our decision to ask Jesus into our life. The journey of dying to ourselves brings its own pain, requiring sacrifices from us, because our soul would much prefer to live by its old, familiar ways. There is pain involved in saying "no" to our flesh, when we are faced with temptations to resort to our previous lifestyles.

It is not us, but God's Holy Spirit that transforms us

By allowing our 'old self' to be broken, we are giving God permission to rule our heart as we say "yes" to His guidance in our life. The more we 'lay down' our painful memories, our prejudices and our old ways, the more we are blessed by the leading of God's Spirit living in us.

God's Holy Spirit is only limited by our limited beliefs

There are no limits in God's kingdom. This means miracles can take place in your life, as you remove doubts of what God can do in you and through you. Our role is to trust God in what He chooses to do in our life. Be willing to change your old beliefs, and expand the borders of your life to be all that God created you to be.

Take the limits off God transforming you, by allowing Him into your deeper self

Scripture: Job 1:21 (NLT)

"I came naked from my mother's womb, and I will be stripped of everything when I die. The Lord gave me everything I had, and the Lord has taken it away. Praise the name of the Lord!"

This Scripture reveals our total dependence on the Lord's provision for us. Job realized this when everything was taken from him, then restored to him even more abundantly by God. Throughout his time of extreme suffering, Job's faith never wavered as he focused on the Lord. This was his journey of being sanctified for God's higher purposes for him, which cost him dearly, yet in the end his reward was far greater than everything he had previously lost.

Secrets of the Hiding Place

Bring Jesus into the moment and everything changes.

Ask Holy Spirit to increase your faith and raise your expectations for answered prayer.

Jehovah-Tsidkenu – The Lord is our Righteousness – Jeremiah 23:6

We cannot be spiritually righteous without God. God's righteousness is a gift given to us because of Jesus' sacrifice, when He took all sin upon Himself at the cross. What does it mean to have righteousness? There are two laws of righteousness, one created by men and the other by God. Man-made laws are limited to our legal systems that do not acknowledge God's laws of righteousness, so are therefore subject to error. When we study God's righteousness, we can be sure there is no partiality or room for error as we seek His justice in our circumstances. Our role in living by the righteousness of God is to allow Him to act on our behalf when correction is needed, to bring about justice in an unjust world. This may not happen according to our expectations and timing, yet IT WILL HAPPEN if we have enough trust and patience to wait on God (believing by faith He will restore His justice to us, because He is a righteous God). I have seen this principle work in my own life over and over again. God always turns wrongs into righteousness for our own good when we allow Him to do so. I have made poor decisions that brought their own negative consequences, yet, whenever I turn to God and ask Him for help in dealing with these consequences, He always brings forth something good from them. This is His righteousness in action!

Jehovah-Jireh – The Lord is our Provider – Genesis 22:14

Where do we turn in our distress? Those who believe, go to God for help. They run to God's "Strong Tower" **(Proverbs 18:10)** for refuge and answers, because God promises to be our strength in trouble. It is important to keep in mind God lives 'in' us, therefore His Strong Tower never leaves us. God's provision (Jehovah-Jireh) already exists within us, meaning we do not have to 'go to' God in our prayers. He is already with us!

Scripture: Psalm 46:1 (NLT)

"God is our refuge and strength, always ready to help in times of trouble."

What separates us from accessing God within us?

I believe there is an incorrect perception of who God is, and how much He loves us, just as we are in this moment. Early in my Christian life I was taught that answers to my prayers depended upon how I behaved, which revealed how 'worthy' I was to attract God's attention. I didn't realize the true nature of God, that He loves me as only He can love, without pre-set conditions required to 'earn' His love. If we are not confident that our prayers will be answered, we are disconnected from the will of God to bless us. Praying without complete trust in God is a form of unbelief, though we may not realize this is so. Our belief in God needs the revelation of who He *really* is, not who we *think* He is. As we expand our understanding of God's true nature, we are actually connecting to His heart. As I observe how believers see God, it appears we have become too familiar in our perceptions of how we see Him. We have lost reverential fear of the magnificent, overpowering awesomeness of our great God who created the Universe. We take the gift of life for granted as we rush through our daily activities, until one day, we realize life is almost over and we wonder what happened to us. We lose touch with the divine gift of life by not focusing on why we were created, to have intimate relationship with our Heavenly Father through Jesus Christ.

Our provision from God is already assured, because of the supreme sacrifice of Christ when He took *all* our sin upon Himself. We lack nothing under the sun, because we have access to ALL of God's provision for us as long as we live. Jehovah-Jireh IS our provision. What we need to do is to connect with the heart of God, and live every moment in thankfulness and gratitude for the amazing gift of life we have been given. Yes, there is suffering in this world, yet as we suffer, God never leaves us nor forsakes us. Ultimately, we become more and more like Him as we join our heartbeat to His divine purposes for us. This is where miracles take place, in the presence of God, in our "hiding place" with Him. This is the "secret place" where the Holy of Holies is revealed to us, where we encounter God Himself. This is called "being in the will of God," as we surrender ourselves to being joined in an intimate relationship with our Creator.

Scripture: Romans 8:16-17 (NLT)

"For His Holy Spirit speaks to us deep in our hearts and tells us that we are God's children. And since we are His children, we will share His treasures – for everything God gives to His Son, Christ, is ours too. But if we are to share His glory, we must also share His suffering."

How do we live in "divine intimacy" with God in our busy lives?

- We position our heart to connect with His heart, by seeking to know Him, and following His Way rather than our own ways.
- We humble ourselves to be unified with His will for us.
- We learn to 'listen' to God's still, quiet voice within us, and choose to be obedient to His guidance.
- We seek His presence in every aspect of our life, by showing honour and respect for Who He is, placing Him first in our priorities.

Why was Moses filled with the glory of God after encountering Him on Mount Sinai, where the skin of his face was shining so brightly, people were afraid to look at Him? He entered God's actual presence and was forever changed. *Each one of us has the opportunity to 'enter' into the Presence of God and be forever changed, from glory to glory. This is our heritage, given to us by God. This is why we were born, to "encounter God" during our lifetime on earth.*

How much do we want God in our life?

We cannot be double-minded in our walk with God. Are we willing to change our old, familiar ways and surrender our pride, our ego, our need to be right and in control? There is only one road to the Shalom peace of God. To walk along this road requires an attitude of self-sacrifice, humility and a willingness to be misunderstood by the people in our life. Moses chose to follow God and was greatly blessed by actually having a living encounter with Him. Once God has touched your heart with His magnificent love, nothing else will ever matter more than living in His presence.

Secret of the Hiding Place

We are given free will by God as a gift. Our responsibility is to use it wisely.

Scripture: Romans 8:38 (NLT)

"I am convinced that nothing can ever separate us from God's love. Death can't, and life can't. The angels can't, and the demons can't. Our fears for today, our worries about tomorrow, and even the powers of hell can't keep God's love away."

THY KINGDOM COME, THY WILL BE DONE IN EARTH AS IT IS IN HEAVEN

As we speak this prayer, we are declaring God's will be done in our life as it is in heaven. Can you see the amazing ramifications of this declaration? You have turned 180 degrees from your old identity, now positioning yourself to receive the glory of God into your heart and life, to be transformed into the image of Jesus Christ. Do not under-estimate the significance of what this means to you personally! Picture yourself standing alone on a beach in the darkness of night, where you can see nothing but reflections of the moon and stars on the ocean. Then visualize yourself turning towards the East as you await the rising of the sun. You see the first rays of light shimmering above the horizon, until the full glory of the sun's orbit shines upon your face; you feel its warmth and life-giving power throughout your body. Can you see yourself receiving heaven's light and glory as God pours Himself into your soul? How would this encounter with God change your life?

- Your mind will be restored and renewed, therefore you will view your problems as opportunities to draw closer to God, rather than seeing them as insurmountable roadblocks along your life's journey.
- You will live with hope in your heart in spite of difficult trials, knowing there are life-lessons to be learned as you 'walk through them to victory.'
- You will celebrate life as you give thanks for your blessings, and take nothing for granted.
- You will live fully in the moment, trusting God to meet your every need as you face each day, with the knowledge He is with you every step of the way.
- You will experience the abiding peace of God that overcomes all fear, as you step into your destiny with confidence.
- You will not be limited by labels people may place upon you, that prevent the full expression of who you really are.
- You will be led by God's wisdom, which protects you from deception and false judgments rooted in the world's value system.

The following Scriptures give a Godly picture of how to view life and be led by wisdom, helping us to do "His will on earth as it is in heaven," by setting our priorities according to what is *really* important. King Solomon wrote these Scriptures from the wisdom he gained after having lived with endless, abundant riches all his life, finally coming to the realization his wealth was not the answer to happiness. He saw the futility of striving for the things of this world, saying: **(Ecclesiastes 3:14-15 - NLT) "And I know that whatever God does is final. Nothing** can be added to it or taken from it. God's purpose in this is that people should fear Him. Whatever exists today and whatever will exist in the future has already existed in the past. For God calls each event back in its turn."

Scripture: Ecclesiastes 3:1-8 (NLT)

"There is a time for everything, a season for every activity under Heaven.
A time to be born and a time to die. A time to plant and a time to harvest.
A time to kill and a time to heal. A time to tear down and a time to rebuild.
A time to cry and a time to laugh. A time to grieve and a time to dance.
A time to scatter stones and a time to gather stones.
A time to embrace and a time to turn away. A time to search and a time to lose.
A time to keep and a time to throw away. A time to tear and a time to mend.
A time to be quiet and a time to speak up. A time to love and a time to hate.
A time for war and a time for peace."

King Solomon's messages can be applied to how we live thousands of years after he wrote these Scriptures, showing us where we need to focus our thoughts and efforts during our allotted time on earth. Do we need to wait for old age to become wise? Hopefully, we are willing to learn from people like Solomon, who appeared to have everything this world has to offer, yet called it all "futile." The wisdom he left behind is to seek God's eternal values by calling "Heaven to Earth" while we can, and not waste our time and energy following futile pursuits, which never satisfy the deep longings of our soul.

What are God's Kingdom Values?

In essence, they are values rooted in love – love for God, love for people, and being so implanted in God's love for us personally, that we see ourselves as His children, worthy of receiving our "Daddy's" love without reservation or question.

Until we see ourselves as being loved and cherished by our Creator, we cannot give unconditional love to others.

We cannot give what we don't have! I believe this is a major cause of conflict in our personal lives, and the world in general. As a whole, we do not understand we were created to love and to be loved. Many of us have problems seeing ourselves as worthy of being loved or lovable to God or people. We see ourselves with jaundiced eyes; we are our own worst critics and sub-consciously, we reject the unconditional love God has for us. We have been taught by society and religion that we must 'earn' the right to be loved and accepted. This view is opposite to Jesus' message. He did not discriminate against anyone who needed help. We, as God's children, are born to become like Jesus, to follow His example. This means to live our lives following the wisdom in **The Lord's Prayer: "Thy will be done on Earth as it is in Heaven."**

Why is it so difficult to love ourselves?

When we observe young children who are being raised in a loving, happy family, what do we see? What draws us in fascination as we watch the innocence, honesty, excitement and joy displayed by children?

- They know they are loved unconditionally.
- They feel safe and secure, with nothing to fear.
- They do not have a need to hide their true feelings.
- They are able to trust without question.
- They feel free to explore and take risks as they seek to discover the world around them.
- They "feel" loved, therefore they respond to love freely.

Why do we lose these childlike qualities as we mature?

We are conditioned by our environment to 'play the game' of survival, to compete for our place in the ladder of progress. We learn to act in certain ways to be 'accepted and acceptable,' to defend ourselves from bullying, jealousy or greed. We are taught to do what is required to find 'approval' from our peers.

Once we have been conditioned by these worldly values, how do we find our way back to feeling good about ourselves, the way we did as children?

We look to God to see ourselves as His son/daughter, we "turn our face" (our heart and thoughts) towards Him, and we become familiar with heavenly values by studying Scripture. We commit to follow God's Ways, and choose to be willing to walk away from (let go of) old ways of thinking, and how we see ourselves.

We choose "life" instead of death!

We 'switch on' to God's truths by plugging in to His power through our thoughts and beliefs.

Scripture: Deuteronomy 30:19 (NLT)

"Today I have given you the choice between life and death, between blessing and curses. I call on heaven and earth to witness the choice you make. Oh, that you would choose life, that you and your descendants might live."

GIVE US THIS DAY OUR DAILY BREAD

What is our "daily bread?"

I like to think it is our "manna from heaven for the moment." In Exodus, God provided manna from heaven for the Israelites as they crossed the wilderness. He did not give them more than they could use daily, because it would spoil in the desert heat. Manna for us is whatever it takes to sustain us in "this day," (including our physical, emotional and spiritual needs). This means we do not have to worry about tomorrow's needs, because it is always "this day" that we live in. Manna is more than our physical nourishment. There is a deeper significance to receiving manna from God to feed our soul. Each day presents new challenges to be met by us, requiring wisdom, strength, patience, hope, commitment, endurance or whatever we are called upon to walk through in our life.

When we ask God to "give us this day our daily bread," keep in mind our existence is very temporary; therefore, our allotted time to discover why we were given the gift of life passes quickly. As we connect to God's eternal values, we think His thoughts, rather than focusing mainly on our own needs. As we do this, we begin the process of transformation, as we 'throw off' the old garment (our old identity), thereby making room for God to reveal Himself in our life. As we trust God to be our daily bread, we are "putting on" a new garment (new identity), which is the 'real' us, the person God created us to be, with unlimited potential to grow and blossom into the "mirror-image" of God.

We limit ourselves by our lack of knowledge and low expectations of who we really are in Christ!

As you pray "Give us this day our daily bread," ask God's Holy Spirit to reveal to you what He wants to give you and teach you in "this day." Ask for His blessings, His presence in all the minūte details of your daily life. Include God in your thoughts as a cherished friend, knowing He cares deeply about who you are, and what happens to you. This way of believing is how you enter your "hiding place" to be in God's presence, regardless of how busy or hectic your life may be. This is how you include God in your life! Every breath you take is a gift from God. As you breathe, think of inhaling God's presence into every cell of your body, every thought you think, every action you take! God gave us the "breath of life" when we were born. He also knows when our last breath will be, when the "breath of life" will leave us **(Job 33:4 - NLT) "For the Spirit of God has made me, and the breath of the Almighty gives me life."**

We are completely dependent on God for our life, yet we are inclined to take it for granted. We waste time as we seek to meet all the demands placed upon us, by striving in our own strength. We can lose our way by becoming distracted by issues that take us out of the will of God for us. We may be tempted to become offended by people, getting frustrated or angry when things don't go our way, or hold grudges and unforgiveness towards people who have hurt us. It is easy to feel inadequate if we compare ourselves to others. Each one of us is subject to thinking and acting negatively, especially under stress, because we are human, but we *can* change if we choose to! We sabotage our true worth and the opportunities to live full, meaningful lives when we are unaware of how God sees us. We may not consciously exclude God, yet when we do not include Him in every aspect of our life, we are turning our backs on Him. Sadly, most of us have not been taught how to find true freedom, joy and happiness by seeking God's presence first, over and above doctrinal teachings. Jesus' message that GOD IS LOVE has become more complicated than it need be. During the times in my life when I experience pain beyond my ability to cope, I call out to God with the following statement: **"Jesus loves me, this I know, because the Bible tells me so."** I find such comfort and strength in these simple, yet profound words that give me hope, even in the darkest places of my human journey. It is God's love that sets us free to soar with Him in high places **(Habakkuk 3:19 - NLT) "The Sovereign Lord is my strength! He will make me as surefooted as a deer and bring me safely over the mountains."**

Only God's divine love can truly set us free to live in "high places" with Him. Only God's love can transform us into the likeness of Jesus Christ, setting our feet on the path of holiness, and birthing new life in us. As we lift our eyes heavenward to see ourselves as divinely linked to God, we gain a new perspective of why we are here on earth for such a short time. This is how we 'connect' to God's plans for us, to live as lovers of all Creation. We are all created to give love and to be loved. Love is the power of God giving life and purpose to each person born. We desecrate this great gift if we turn away from God and what He represents to us **(James 1:17-18 - NLT) "Whatever is good and perfect comes to us from God above, who created all heaven's lights. In His goodness He chose to make us His own children by giving us His true word. And we, out of all creation, became His choice possession."**

Secrets of the Hiding Place

Plug into your unlimited potential by aligning your thoughts with how God sees you.

When we choose God, we experience His serenity. God's serenity pervades our spirit, as if we are already living in Heaven.

Scripture: Matthew 6:25-27 (NLT)

"So I tell you, don't worry about everyday life – whether you have enough food, drink and clothes. Look at the birds. They don't need to plant or harvest or put food in barns because your Heavenly Father feeds them. And you are far more valuable to Him than they are. Can all your worries add a single moment to your life? Of course not!"

If we could truly grasp the full meaning of the above Scripture, how would this change our life, our approach and attitudes towards how we think and live?

Firstly, what would our life look like if we really understood and accepted what God is saying to us in these words? Let us look at some of the hidden messages involved in this Scripture.

FEAR OF THE UNKNOWN

We would be free from the fear of being without provision. We would be able to trust God's Word, knowing that even when trials challenge us, our circumstances will ultimately be blessed by God as we "come into agreement" with His promises for us. As we 'take hold' of our thoughts by focusing on these promises, we consciously align ourselves with His good will for us, trusting in positive outcomes from our efforts.

DOUBT AND WORRY

These negative thought patterns remove us from God's best for us. When we worry and doubt, we are subconsciously declaring we don't believe we are worthy of receiving positive outcomes in our life (regardless of how hard we may work to improve our circumstances). Worry and doubt give rein (control) to negative outcomes, as we literally declare curses over ourselves by giving in to these thought patterns. Thoughts are constantly flowing through our minds randomly. Unless we harness and discipline them, we cannot experience true peace.

What do you speak over your life?

Step One

Try the following exercise to reveal the thoughts you think and the words you speak for one day. Carry a notebook and pen with you throughout the day, and write down your thoughts and the words you speak to monitor yourself. Be objective, as though this is a school assignment. Be specific in recording what you think and say, so that you can accurately assess your thoughts and spoken words, especially regarding yourself. Once you have done this, you will be more aware of how you really see yourself.

Step Two

Set a goal for yourself to change your negative thoughts and words to positive ones. Be the "gatekeeper" of your thoughts and spoken words. Whenever you think or say something negative, consciously 'send it away' by saying out loud:

"You are a liar! Get out and don't come back. You are not welcome!"

Then speak the following words:

"I choose to believe in good things. I replace this lie with God's truth and what He says about me! I believe God loves me and wants the best for me. I am loved and worthy of receiving:

,,,"
(fill in your specific needs and requests here).

Then thank God out loud for what He is doing in your life, and what He has done for you in the past. Live with an attitude of gratitude from your heart. Be grateful for small blessings, to pave the way for greater blessings in the future.

Think about what you are thinking about, and the words you speak over your life

As we enter our "hiding place" in God, we are actually harnessing the negative, undisciplined thoughts entering our mind, choosing instead to listen to the "still, quiet voice" within us, which is God's Holy Spirit speaking to us. It is God's will for us to be guided by His Spirit. We need to make ourselves available to hear what He is saying to us. When we enter into communication with Him in our spirit, we connect with His Kingdom in Heaven as we speak these words: **"Give us this day our daily bread."**

FORGIVE US OUR TRESPASSES, AS WE FORGIVE THOSE WHO TRESPASS AGAINST US

The word trespass is so descriptive, painting a picture of something or someone 'trespassing' the healthy boundaries we need around us to keep us safe. This principle also applies to how we treat others. Do we 'trespass' their boundaries by having unreasonable expectations they cannot fulfill? There are many different ways we can trespass against others, such as being thoughtless, unkind, not reaching out to help those in need, being inconsiderate, even in minor ways. To trespass is to stomp on others' dignity, and there is no justification for this type of behavior. I know I am guilty of being thoughtless as I look back over my life. Sadly, we cannot change our past behavior, but we can now ask God to help us bless the people we encounter in our everyday life. I ask God in prayer every morning to help me be a blessing to someone each day. We need to forgive ourselves for when we trespassed against others, and we also need to forgive all the people who have trespassed against us. This can be deep work in our heart, for some of the emotional wounding from the past needs "Holy Spirit surgery" to mend our brokenness. We need to forgive ourselves, as well as anyone who has hurt us, in order to come to a place of restoration and peace in our soul. Each one of us has our own story of what needs to be forgiven and overcome. Jesus has shown us "the Way" to healing and ultimately, to transformation, by how He lived His life on earth. We cannot fully heal in our own strength and wisdom.

The Lord's Prayer is a foundational guide, based upon Scriptural principles, to show us what we need to do to live transformed lives. What we do with these guiding principles is our individual responsibility. We are ultimately responsible for our own choices. Jesus has paved the road for us to follow in His footsteps. When we follow Him on this road, we will be blessed, protected, guided, comforted and healed. We will experience deep, abiding peace. We will be led by Godly wisdom. We will encounter miracles, healings, hope, joy, contentment and abiding peace. Most importantly, we will experience the presence of God! Should we choose to divert from the road Jesus walked, we step away from the covering of God, therefore we are 'uncovered' and vulnerable to the temptations of the world. Temptations come in many forms, and can be very subtle as we give in to the values we see manifested around us. The closer we draw to the presence of God, the more revelation we will have about what we should avoid.

LEAD US NOT INTO TEMPTATION, BUT DELIVER US FROM EVIL

Does God lead us into temptation? I don't believe so. My personal understanding of this part of The Lord's Prayer is our request to God to give us discernment, to know His will when we are faced with temptation. Because God has given us free will, we have choices as to what decisions we make, good or evil, positive or negative, helpful or harmful. When we pray these words, we are asking God to protect us from anything that could harm us, to "deliver us from evil" as we make decisions each and every day of our lives. Our decisions are the 'pivotal point' of whatever road we choose to walk on (live) during our life journey. We are constantly confronted with temptations that require decisions from us to 'accept' or 'reject' them in our conscious thoughts. This is why we need God in our life, to give us inner discernment, through His Holy Spirit. If we do not recognize our need for God and His guidance, we are ruled by our feelings, thus we are subject to the fluctuations of whatever we are experiencing emotionally. We cannot live a stable existence governed solely by our personal feelings. Emotions play a necessary part in our lives, yet when they are undisciplined, they can become a hard taskmaster.

Do we want to be ruled by our fluctuating emotions or, do we want peace, stability and guidance from our inner compass, God's Holy Spirit living in us?

Our emotions are a gift from God, to be harnessed for our pleasure when we choose to be led by His "reins of wisdom," just as a race-horse is governed by its trainer, who controls its reins. This is how God "delivers us from evil" to protect us from being harmed by the unwise decisions we may make.

FOR THINE IS THE KINGDOM, AND THE POWER AND THE GLORY, FOR EVER AND EVER, AMEN

Are we governed by God's kingdom values, or the values of the world?

What are God's kingdom values?

- Abiding peace (lasting rather than temporary)
- Unconditional love (no strings attached)
- Forgiveness
- Mercy and trust
- No judgment towards others
- Freedom from offenses
- Wisdom and God's justice
- Life everlasting
- Freedom in our heart
- Healing of body and emotions
- Provision and abundance
- Creativity fully expressed
- Fairness and honour towards each other
- Joy and hope
- Divine justice
- Redemption
- Sanctification (set apart for a special purpose)

What are some of the world's values as we know them?

- Ruled by the laws of mankind alone (not God's laws)
- Injustice (discrimination based upon man's concept of justice)
- Personal prejudices
- Conflict without resolutions

- Class distinctions
- Mistrust
- All forms of abuse towards others
- Jealousy and covetousness
- Religious wars rather than God's love
- Suspicion and envy
- Fear
- Lack of balance causing disharmony
- Overindulgence in our appetites
- Insecurities in all their forms
- Emotional highs and lows
- Unhealthy habits with all their consequences
- Dysfunctional behaviors
- Selfishness

Why is the world so far removed from God's values?

Because we have turned away from God, with the mistaken belief we are choosing 'freedom' as we separate ourselves from who God is, and what He means to us. There is a misconception that we lose our freedoms by coming under the banner of God's values - **"Thy Kingdom come, Thy will be done on Earth as it is in Heaven."** In our desire for freedom we have become so self-focused, we have lost true liberty; meaning, we have walked away from the kingdom values our Western civilizations were founded upon. We all know what they are: Life, liberty and the pursuit of happiness for all under God's dominion. The results of living separated from God's heavenly values are self-evident. We have removed ourselves from God's protective covering, from His grace freely given to those whose hearts are turned towards Him. When we honour God in our heart, we embrace His kingdom values over the world's lifestyle.

Our world is spinning off its axis, not only physically but also spiritually. The Lord's Prayer shows us what we need to change, both individually and collectively as we move forward. We each have the responsibility in our own life to do what we can to return to God's kingdom values. This is not difficult! All it takes is a heartfelt decision to say "YES" to God, to turn the 'axis' of our thoughts towards Him and away from our old ways of thinking. When we make this decision, we are choosing to turn our hearts towards the Light of God's kingdom, thus turning away from the darkness we see around us. When we do this, we carry His Light within us, which changes the atmosphere wherever we go (because His Light shines through us, and is reflected in our thoughts, attitudes and actions). As carriers of God's Light, we bring "heaven to earth" like mirrors shining light into darkness. God's glory is revealed through righteousness (right thinking and acts), as we position our hearts towards Him. Picture yourself as a lantern. The fire within you is waiting to be lit by God when you allow yourself to be led by His Holy Spirit, who is the oil in your lantern. You yourself are not the Light, but without you (His lantern), God cannot shine through you to bless others.

When you think about Creation, nothing could exist without the Light of God, because all life is dependent upon light. Light is evidence that God is real. We don't like to admit our dependency upon God, yet without His light there would be total darkness over the earth. Light is the source of ALL Creation in God's divine plan for earth, and because mankind has dominion over all the earth, we profoundly influence the quality of life upon it. If we could see ourselves as carriers of light to reflect God's glory, we would assume greater responsibility for our role to bring about harmony and balance to our environment.

What would this look like in our life?

- We would govern our thought life to seek beauty, rather than focus on discords manifested around us.
- We would honour each other as equal carriers of the life God has given us.
- We would begin each day asking for God's guidance.
- We would assume our responsibility to be an instrument of peace.
- We would value each precious moment as a gift from God.
- We would refuse to participate in conflict and others' prejudices against the differences in people.
- We would take a stand against injustices inflicted upon innocent people.

God's light increases within us as we align ourselves to His values. Our "inner vision" (spirit) is magnified as we place more importance on who God is, and what He stands for in our life. The burning wick within us is 'turned up' to shed more light into dark places, bringing increased life to the atmosphere around us. This light is emitted as a ripple effect of light waves to profoundly influence wherever it shines.

What would the world look like if we could each take responsibility to do our part in bringing heaven to earth?

- Conflict and wars would diminish.
- Strife between people would be replaced by love and understanding.
- Earth would gradually be transformed into the Garden of Eden as God originally created it to be.
- Sicknesses and diseases would be replaced with divine health, as we made choices to live in harmony with God's laws. (Medical science is aware that most diseases are caused by an acidic environment in our bodies, largely brought on by stress). As we come into harmony with God, His healing power restores balance to our body and soul.

We are a long way from seeing what I describe here, yet I believe this is God's ultimate plan for us. As we each choose to live by His laws and principles, we will make a positive difference in establishing some inroads towards achieving more balance and harmony personally, and also in our environment.

Secret of the Hiding Place

The love of God dispels all darkness in its wake.

SYNOPSIS OF THE LORD'S PRAYER

Praying to God is an act of communing with Him, coming into agreement with God's will for us. In **John 14:12-13** Jesus tells His disciples that "whatever we ask in His name can be accomplished upon earth."

We are told in Scripture to pray on the basis of whom Jesus is, and it will be so. Faith is being confident that whatever Jesus did upon earth can be accomplished through us, as we pray to God our Father, in the name of Jesus Christ.

Our purpose as believers is to establish upon earth what already exists in heaven

We have been given authority to "call in" to our lives, through our believing prayers, everything God has promised us in Scripture. When we do this, we are decreeing that whatever is already established in heaven will be established on earth. If we don't do this, it won't happen! The key to accessing God's kingdom was transferred to us when Jesus Christ died on the cross. As we pray in Jesus' name, we are decreeing God's will upon earth. Our mind needs to be set to God's compass as we pray, rather than to our negative expectations.

Scripture: Matthew 18:18 (NLT)

"Whatever you prohibit on earth is prohibited in Heaven, and whatever you allow on earth is allowed in Heaven." Another way of explaining this Scripture is: "Lord, whatever you say is legal in heaven, let it be legal upon earth."

Secrets of the Hiding Place

Don't ask God for what Jesus has already paid the price for. We have access to the gates of Heaven by believing this is so.

We tap into Heaven by tapping into who God created us to be.

REFLECTIONS

- How would you describe the true meaning of The Lord's Prayer?

- Write down some of the many names of the Lord, along with their meanings.

- What are some of the qualities needed in us to become conformed into God's image?

- How do we access the process of transformation in our personal life?

- What separates us from accessing God within us?

- How do we live in "divine intimacy" with God in our busy lives?

- What do you speak over your life? (Follow the steps written in this chapter to help you identify how you see yourself).

- What are some of God's kingdom values?

- As a carrier of the Light of God, what differences can you make on earth by following His leading?

Chapter Ten

THE CROSS AND WHAT IT REPRESENTS TO US

*D*o we really grasp the life changing significance of what was accomplished at the cross when Jesus died to conquer all sin?

Scripture: Colossians 1:19-22 (NLT)

"For God in all His fullness was pleased to live in Christ, and by Him God reconciled everything to Himself. He made peace with everything in heaven and on earth by means of His blood on the cross. As a result, He has brought you into the very presence of God, and you are holy and blameless as you stand before Him without a single fault."

How does God see you?

God sees you through the lenses of His Son Jesus, meaning He sees you as His perfect son/daughter, without blemish. God sees you as justified, meaning you have been restored from everything that harmed you before you asked Jesus into your heart. You have been forgiven of all iniquity (feeling less than what you were created to be), meaning you should not carry the burdens of shame, regrets, condemnation, guilt or anything that steals your true identity, and thus your peace.

You have been made righteous in the eyes of God, because Jesus took all unrighteousness upon Himself at the cross. You are righteous, but do you see yourself in this way? This gift of righteousness has been freely given to you. Have you received this gift? If you have, you have come into agreement with how God sees you. Does your life reflect this truth? If you know you are righteous, forgiven, and justified, what would this look like in how you see yourself and how you live? Perhaps this question can be explained more clearly by sharing how my life has changed as I sought to understand the true significance of Jesus dying on the cross.

I felt the weight of the world on my shoulders while I was dealing with the effects of abuse from childhood. It felt as though I was walking under heavy water as I struggled with low self-esteem, shame, guilt and an overwhelming sense of hopelessness. I realize now that I believed lies about who I am in God's view. I didn't know that I could break free from these heavy burdens by coming to the cross, spiritually speaking, to exchange my pain for all those things Jesus died to give me. I had to do this myself! No-one else could do this for me! I am still receiving new revelations of what this "Divine Exchange" really means. As we lay down every burden we carry (our daily challenges) at the foot of the cross, (meaning we consciously surrender personal control of our circumstances to God), in effect we are saying:

"Lord Jesus, I give to you all these false burdens I have been carrying (worrying about, holding onto in my thoughts and feelings), and now choose to release them to You. I understand that all these things I lay down and surrender to You are not mine to carry! I believe that You have already paid the ultimate price, that I do not need to pay the price again by striving in my own strength. That is a lie I believed, and now I come into agreement that You died to set me free, so that I can live the transformed life promised to me. I now declare I have received Your gift of grace, as I step into all the promises of God. In Jesus' name I pray. Amen."

This declaration to God is a process of changing (transforming) self-beliefs to align with how God sees you. The more we believe these truths, the deeper we enter into God's presence in our "hiding place" in Him. In my own walk with God, I now find I can come into a deep awareness of His presence by just thinking about Him. We need to be aware of the battle of random, undirected thoughts that can distract us, taking us out of the presence of God when we focus solely on circumstances around us. We need to be aware and disciplined in our thought life, beginning each day choosing God's Way over the roller coaster of our feelings and negative thoughts. *It is important to remind ourselves of the futility of carrying the burdens Jesus paid the price for.* When we keep 'picking up' the burdens we have given to Jesus in prayer, we step away from His presence in our heart. By doing this, we are choosing confusion and chaos over God's peace, joy and tranquility in our soul. Worry does not prevent tomorrow's sorrows; it steals the strength we need for today.

The cross Jesus died upon was the demarcation line between death and life, and still is. We choose, by our beliefs, which side of this line we will live.

- Darkness or light
- Ignorance or wisdom
- Denial or acceptance
- Scepticism or Truth
- Torment or peace
- Hate or love
- Imprisonment or freedom

We imprison ourselves by how we see ourselves!

How do we connect with God, meaning, how do we "experience" Him?

We need the revelation of what the cross really means to us, by understanding more deeply what was truly accomplished when Jesus allowed Himself to become a Living Sacrifice for all mankind. Jesus Christ took upon Himself ALL the sin of the world. What does this mean? It means He paid the ultimate price for sin so that mankind can experience all the promises of God as a free gift. What does God promise us?

Scripture: 2 Peter 3:4 (NLT)

"As we know Jesus better, his divine power gives us everything we need for living a godly life. He has called us to receive his own glory and goodness! And by that same mighty power, he has given us all of his rich and wonderful promises. He has promised that you will escape the decadence all around you caused by evil desires and that you will share in his divine nature."

God promises us healing from sickness and disease. He promises us comfort in our distress, strength in our weakness, hope when all hope seems lost, joy when trials threaten to overwhelm us, and peace during our stormy circumstances.

How do we access His promises to us?

We think beyond the box of our circumstances, and step into new beliefs about God's unconditional faithfulness. We do this by re-programming our mind to think new thoughts, aligned with who God says He is: The God of unlimited possibilities! As we gain insight into what Christ accomplished for us by dying on the cross, we expand our mind to accept what He really did for us. He took ALL sin, ALL evil, ALL sickness, ALL lacks, ALL mental disorders, ALL hate, greed, selfishness, despair, suicidal thoughts, addictions and ALL ignorance.

What did He give us in return for taking all these things upon Himself?

He gave us freedom from all things that represent evil on earth. He gave unconditional love, acceptance, peace, wisdom, joy and hope to all who believe in Him. He gave us access to our heavenly Father in Heaven. In doing this, He opened "the Way" for us to receive all of God's promises. Can you meditate on this for a moment? Do you understand the amazing significance of this truth? We now have the opportunity to receive everything God holds for us, because of Jesus' sacrifice of Himself on the cross. How do we access these promises? By believing what was accomplished through His death and resurrection. It is helpful to understand the spiritual message of what the cross means to us by explaining the ceremony of baptism, and what takes place within us when we are baptized.

Firstly, we are immersed under water. This means we are submerging (dying) to our old self and all that we were, so that when we are lifted up out of the water, we covenant (agree) with God to leave our sinful nature behind. Spiritually speaking, our new nature joins with Jesus to be resurrected with Him into our new life.

What does this mean to us?

It means we are "new creatures" with all the attributes, blessings and character of Jesus planted in our spirit when we receive God's Holy Spirit. Our life then becomes a journey of "walking with Jesus" along the road that leads to our transformation, to become the fulfillment of the plans God has destined for us.

What does this look like in our life?

When we pray for healing, we do not need to beg God for help, because He has already given healing to us through Jesus' death and resurrection. What we need to do to receive healing is to declare:

"I am already healed by the stripes of Jesus. I choose to walk in this healing now, by faith, believing that it has been accomplished in my life."

Even though we may not see the physical evidence of our healing immediately, as we continue to declare and believe for it, we are coming into agreement with God that we will be healed. This may look different from our personal expectations. Our role is to 'expect' healing and be open to the many ways God uses to heal us. In my personal experience, I have found God brings people into my life whom He uses to help my healing process. I always give thanks to the wonderful people who are gifted in the many therapies available to help people get well. The key is to *believe* in your heart you will be healed. Continue aligning your thoughts with God's promises to heal and bless you. Always remember that everything Jesus is resides within you, waiting for you to connect, through your faith, with this truth. This same principle applies to whatever your needs may be. *Let your prayers be declarations filled with expectations of what you know God will do for you.*

Secret of the Hiding Place

To experience healing, allow God's Word to make a home in your heart and mind.

How do we enter into a deeper connection with God?

We have the opportunity to *know* God, to experience His presence in our life. How do we receive this life-changing gift? We open our heart to the limitless life God offers us when we are willing to repent for holding rebellion, pride, stubbornness, or anything separating us from Him, and lay them down at the cross. As long as we hold onto these qualities, we are not open to receiving God's promises and blessings. Our heart is closed like an iron door that locks us into our self-imposed prisons. We cannot receive true freedom until we open the door of our heart, and repent for our lack of belief in God. A repentant heart is the *key* to unlocking the door that holds us prisoners to darkness.

The Cross of Jesus represents the door to enter into God's presence!

When we lay down our selfish, prideful ways at the cross, what we are doing is turning the key to open the door of our heart, so that God's Holy Spirit can increase in our spirit. The key to experiencing God's presence lies with us, as we choose to use this key of repentance.

What takes place within us when we take all our cares to the Cross of Jesus?

- God's peace invades our soul.

- We are released from the burdens that cause heaviness in our heart.
- Hope for our future is birthed in our soul.
- We experience a new awareness of belonging to something bigger than ourselves.
- We "enter the door" into God's kingdom, where all things are possible.
- We have access to the power of God through our beliefs, as we pray in Jesus' name. This means we can receive healing, provision and all the blessings God promises us in His Word.
- We experience new freedom in our heart and soul.
- Our true identity is restored and revealed to us.

Freedom is a choice, based upon whether we receive what Christ died to give us, or whether we reject His gift of grace. There are no conditions placed on receiving this gift, other than believing God's Word that it is yours for the asking, because of Jesus' sacrifice of Himself. You ask! Then you receive, because you asked. Once we 'cross the line' established by Jesus Christ's death and resurrection, we then begin our journey of intimacy with God as we seek to know His true nature. This life journey is endless, like an eternal dance as we follow His leading. In time we become attuned to Holy Spirit within us, sensing, through our thoughts and feelings, what God is communicating to lead us to our eternal destiny. What this means is not so much about our performance, as it is about living according to His will as we follow Him.

What is meant by "the position of our heart?"

There are two answers to this question.

We can think we are following God's leading in our thoughts, as we endeavour to live up to what we believe is expected of us to please God.

Or

We can see ourselves as a little child who is totally dependent on parental guidance and protection for all our needs. This means we know we cannot survive without their care for us. As children of God, we are as dependent upon Him as we were in childhood with our earthly parents.

The first interpretation is based on 'religious laws' from the Old Testament, whereby we see God from our head knowledge of who we think He is. When we think this way, we base our progress and close connection with God on our own efforts (pride), taking personal credit for whatever we do to receive God's approval.

The second approach is when we give God permission to "mold us into His image" as we surrender ourselves to this process. We cannot draw close to Him unless we see Him as our "Father in Heaven" who guides us into all He has for us. We do this knowing we are incomplete without Him leading us. This is the state of being open and receptive to whom God created us to be, meaning we have an open heart turned towards Him.

When we are willing to let old memories be replaced with how God sees us, it is like turning our face towards the sunshine (living light), to receive the gift of life Jesus died to give us. The cross represents the difference between life and death, or God's promises versus old memories, where our face is turned towards darkness (the past).

How do we assess our real value?

We need to understand our place on earth, and why we were created. It is imperative we realize we are an integral part of a divine plan in Creation. We need to 'connect the dots' of our physical existence with our spiritual self, that is, our link to God. There is a huge gap separating mankind from God. What is this gap? It is our mistaken belief that our existence begins and ends with our finite years spent on earth. How can we discover our real value when our focus is limited to who the world says we are? It is in this place we are tossed and turned by circumstances that limit our potential to "fly like an eagle" **(Isaiah 40:31)** as we merely exist in a chicken pen.

How do we step into who God says we are?

We lift our eyes to 'look up' to Heaven's kingdom and see ourselves as eagles.

How do we do this?

We position ourselves in our thoughts and heart to choose God's Way for us. We make a fundamental shift, by looking up instead of down, as we turn towards Living Light instead of darkness (circumstances). We are beings made up of three parts, body, soul and spirit. We are given a body to house our soul (mind, will and emotions), to serve us during our lifetime. Our spirit is the center of who we are in this amazing journey of life. Our spirit is the part of us that connects with God's Spirit living within us, our divine connection to Him. When we die, our body has served its purpose, so is no longer needed. We have the choice to live our life confined to meeting our personal needs alone, (meaning we do not seek God and His divine purposes for us on earth), or, we can use our mind, will and emotions (our soul) to pursue God, and align ourselves with His kingdom purposes for us on earth.

Keys to reflect upon to remind us of who we are in God's kingdom

- Worldly values remove us from God's presence.
- You have a spiritual identity as well as a human identity.
- You have an eternal destiny – do not squander this divine gift from God.
- Just BE! Don't strive.
- Our outer life (visible) is works oriented. Our inner life (invisible) is the secret place where our thoughts, hopes and desires exist. Do not neglect your inner life.
- Our soul is created to reveal our need for God. Nothing outside of God will fulfill this inner need in us.
- As you give yourself away to bless others, your soul will be satisfied.
- Our spirit and soul are the eternal parts of us. Our body is the temporary home of our spirit and soul.

Scripture: 1 Corinthians 2:9-10 (NLT)

"No eye has seen, nor ear has heard, and no mind has imagined what God has prepared for those who love Him. But we know these things because God has revealed them to us by His Spirit, and His Spirit searches out everything and shows us even God's deep secrets."

This Scripture reveals to us it is God's Holy Spirit that transforms us from mere man to step into our Godly destiny as "eagles." This is how we see the 'bigger picture' from God's perspective. When this happens, we are forever changed from comparing ourselves to others; instead, we see ourselves as part of the awesome plans God has destined for us.

What changes within us when we see ourselves as divinely chosen by God?

- We gain a new understanding that whatever circumstances we are faced with, they are part of the bigger picture that God will ultimately reveal to us.
- We live with the knowledge we were created for God's divine plans for us, therefore we do not lose the value of who we are during times of testing and losses.
- We see others as valuable, rather than needing to compete with them.
- We live with acceptance that "all things work together for good," which brings peace and rest to our soul.
- We become aware of how God reveals Himself to us, as we observe hidden meanings and lessons behind everyday events.
- We lose the fear of stepping out of our comfort zones, to explore new ways of living.
- We enter a world of unlimited potential, where doors of opportunity open for us to participate in.
- We discover hidden qualities within us that open up our vision, to explore the world and become partakers of God's promises.

- We dare to dream big dreams as the shutters of fear and doubt fall away from us.
- As partakers of God's promises, we become a beacon of His Light to bring hope to others in their brokenness.
- We live rooted and grounded in kingdom principles, which give us strength and wisdom in the storms of life.
- We see life with the "eyes of our heart," enabling us to live beyond the physical limitations of our five senses.
- As we view life with the eyes of our heart, we see beauty in unexpected places as God reveals His mysteries to us.
- We are able to live more completely in the present moment, to participate fully in the exquisiteness of each precious season of our life.
- We move closer to the perfection of God's love for us.

The true message of the cross is to be willing to die to our 'old self,' the person we used to be before we knew Jesus. We need to be willing to change our self-image and let go of old limitations we placed on ourselves, or had placed upon us by others. As we replace our old values with the wonderful gifts Jesus died to give us, we enter into the miraculous transformation from who we believed we were, to becoming people who are set free to soar and fly as an eagle, with the promise of New Life from God.

Secret of the Hiding Place

Awaken your spiritual senses to live beyond limitations stamped on your heart by fear.

THE SUPERNATURAL LIFESTYLE

Can we live a supernatural lifestyle in a materialistic world?

Earlier in this book I wrote about the invisible world of spirit being more real than what we see with our five senses. Do we limit the movement of God in our lives by denying the existence of supernatural happenings? I believe we do. The longer I live, the more I realize some things cannot be explained by our worldly logic. God reveals Himself to us through His Creation, which is a mystery. When my children were born and placed in my arms for the first time, I was overwhelmed by their perfection and uniqueness. I was in awe of the miracle of new life formed from a tiny seed planted in my womb, which had nothing to do with my own ability to create a child. I was merely the vessel God chose for them to be formed by Him. The creation of a child is one way God reveals Himself to us. He is a creative God with no limitations. Once we position ourselves to seek the many ways God manifests Himself to us, our spiritual eyes are opened to the invisible, supernatural world we live in. We can tap into this world as we attune our spirit-self (God within us), to 'hear' and 'see' the awesome mysteries available for us to discover.

Listening to our inner spirit can be developed and fine-tuned to focus more on the invisible world around us, where we see beyond the obvious physical manifestations our five senses observe. You can call it intuition, sensitivity, inner knowing, psychic awareness, prophetic insight or unexplained miracles to try to explain the supernatural, which I believe most people can relate to in some way. In Old Testament times, seeing angels and hearing the voice of God was accepted as normal. This changed when Constantine combined Roman thinking with Christianity, which, combined with Greek logic, overruled the importance of acknowledging supernatural happenings in people's lives. There is no denying the hunger in people to understand the supernatural world. Modern Christianity often misses the fundamental need to embrace this invisible, supernatural world around us. How else can miracles be explained? What about the signs and wonders written about in Scripture? Jesus performed many miracles, signs and wonders for all to see, not for His glory, but to reveal what is available to those who believe. Do we believe we can do what Jesus did when we pray and decree God's truths over the brokenhearted, sick and disillusioned people around us? Do we really believe God's supernatural power can be released through our prayers? Are we truly walking in faith, or do we limit God by our limited beliefs in what He can do for those we pray for? Are we able to grab a hold of the concept that God can do **anything** we ask in Jesus' name. This happened in Jesus' time on earth. WHY NOT NOW?

178

Scripture: John 14:12-13 (NLT)

"The truth is, anyone who believes in Me will do the same works I have done, and even greater works, because I am going to be with the Father. You can ask for anything in My name, and I will do it, because the works of the Son brings glory to the Father."

We need to take our preconceived blinkers off our spiritual eyes. We need new boldness, openness and trust to pursue and re-discover the hidden mysteries God holds for us in the invisible, supernatural world we have available to us; (if only we will choose to see beyond our physical senses). The message of the cross is well explained in the above Scripture. When we really believe Jesus' words, we step into the Resurrected life He died to give us.

How do we develop our spiritual senses?

The more we seek hidden meanings behind what we observe with our physical senses, the more attuned we become to 'seeing' with our spiritual eyes. The key is to continually "ask" in our thoughts for insight into what lies behind the obvious. God's Holy Spirit in us is "all-knowing," therefore we need to discover for ourselves how to access (listen to) Holy Spirit. We can develop our spiritual eyes by using our 'spiritual muscles' the way we build up our physical muscles to become strong. The more we ask, meditate and study God's Word, the more finely tuned we become to see spiritually. Jesus Christ applied this principle to perfection by always asking His Father in Heaven for guidance, rather than acting on His own. We can do this too, by continually asking Holy Spirit for divine insight and guidance in our thoughts and prayers. As we "go to the Father" by listening to Holy Spirit within us, we enter the realm of God's Kingdom. This is how we live in God's will. We do nothing outside of His will as we obey God, by listening to what He communicates to us. As we surrender our will to be attuned and obedient to God's leading, we are transformed into the likeness of Jesus. This is how we enter into God's "supernatural lifestyle."

Steps to developing our spiritual senses

- Spend time with God as you seek to know Him **(Romans 10:17).**
- Memorize Scriptures that are meaningful to you, so that you can reflect on them throughout each day.
- Be objective about what triggers negative responses in you. When this occurs, pray to Holy Spirit to be guided in how Jesus would respond to similar situations.
- Do not allow pride to prevent you from listening to God.
- Make wise choices for yourself by asking for God's guidance before making any decisions.
- Follow peace in your heart over impulsive choices.
- When you meet people, ask God in prayer to give you His insight into who they really are, and what their needs may be; (the more you do this, the greater understanding you will develop to "see the gold" within them, rather than merely seeing their outward appearance).
- Make your needs known to God in prayer. Seek His guidance and ask for help as you experience trials and challenges **(Philippians 4.6).**
- Be continually thankful to God for what He is doing in your life.
- Focus on the 'bigger picture' in your circumstances, and be aware God uses "all things for good" **(Romans 8:28).**
- Never give up! God hasn't given up on you. He sees you as complete in Him, not the mistakes you make along the way.
- Stop being hard on yourself.
- Allow yourself to receive God's love for you.
- Do what you can and give the rest to God.
- Enjoy the journey of discovering God's presence in every area of your life.
- Assume personal responsibility for who and what you believe.

Scripture: 1 Corinthians 1:21-22 (NLT)

"It is God who gives us the ability to stand firm for Christ. He has commissioned us, and He has identified us as His own by placing

the Holy Spirit in our hearts as the first installment of everything He will give us."

The Supernatural lifestyle

- Miracles happen (there is much evidence that they do).
- Spontaneous healings occur beyond medical science.
- Angels are real (can you recall when you felt something or someone protected you from a possible accident or calamity)?
- Have you thought of someone, then met or heard from them unexpectedly?
- Have your prayers been answered when all else failed?
- Have you been moved by instinct to make decisions that produced good results?

The world has coined a phrase it calls 'coincidence' when happenings occur that defy logic. In other words, supernatural phenomenon is placed in a box called 'chance' to explain the unexplainable. This way of thinking reduces mankind to the lowest common denominator, meaning we see ourselves as mere pawns of circumstances in God's Creation, which leads to a sense of hopelessness and despair.

Secrets of the Hiding Place

We are given life to have relationship with God and each other, to be a blessing and overcome evil.

You do not need to prove yourself to God. He knows you and loves you as you are.

REFLECTIONS

- What did Jesus accomplish when He died on the Cross?

- Ask yourself this question: "Do I see myself as God sees me?"

- How do we connect with God, meaning, how do we 'experience' Him in our heart?

- How do we access God's promises for us?

- What is meant by "the position of your heart" in your relationship with God?

- How do we 'step into' who God says we are?

- Write down some of the keys written about in this chapter to remind you of who you are in God's kingdom.

- What changes within us when we see ourselves as divinely chosen by God?

- Describe what you understand about living a supernatural lifestyle.

- How do we develop our "spiritual senses?" (Refer to what is written in this chapter).

Chapter Eleven

THE GIFT OF PEACE

Scripture: Romans 5:1 (NLT)

"Therefore, since we have been made right in God's sight by faith, we have peace with God because of what Jesus Christ our Lord has done for us."

We are rarely free from circumstances that threaten to steal our peace. It often feels like a war zone between chaos and the need for peace, as we endeavour to deal with the roller coaster of life. The challenge is to remain calm in our thoughts and feelings, when it feels as if we could lose our emotional stability, while situations beyond our control sweep over us.

How can we win the war between chaos and peace in our mind?

By choosing God's peace through our faith!

How do we do this?

We establish the mindset of seeking His presence as a lifestyle every moment of our life. This means we "include" God in every breath we take, in every waking minute, in every thought we think, in every decision we make. This is not difficult to achieve! We make our life difficult by focusing primarily on the world outside of God's domain. We complicate our life by thinking wrong thoughts, as we navigate through the minefields of our existence. We fall into the trap of excessive reasoning, trying to solve our problems in our own limited ways. We take on the role of 'playing God' as we try to figure out the answers to every problem we encounter (as well as problems of people close to us). We become entwined in the complexities of people's issues, needs and judgments, which actually are none of our business. We try to 'fix' situations to give us some sense of control, which is an illusion, because what we are actually doing is causing more confusion for ourselves, and for others, when we interfere. Our role is to pray and ask God to show how He would lead us to help. The old saying: "Let go, let God" is profound. When we follow the leading of God's Holy Spirit, we are choosing the way of Wisdom rather than following our feelings. When we pray to God for guidance, we need to step aside from our thoughts and emotions to be quiet, to connect in our spirit with His Spirit, and rest in His promise of abiding peace when we choose His Way. This is how we release our heavy burdens and enter **"His peace that passes all understanding" (John 14:27).**

What is peace and what are its benefits to us?

- Peace is the gift of grace from God
- Peace is the elixir of love in its many forms
- Peace brings healing to our heart, mind and emotions
- Peace is worth whatever we have to sacrifice to experience it
- Peace is a jewel of great value, over and above anything the world offers

When we choose to live in peace, we are actually protecting ourselves from chaos and turmoil. There is a well-known saying: "Divide and conquer." Division separates us from peace. When we allow our thoughts to become confused by allowing our feelings to rule us, we become separated from the peace of God, causing us to become vulnerable to the negative effects of stress in our life. We cannot be 'double-minded' and experience peace within us. If you are established in knowing who you are in the eyes of God, you cannot be swayed from living by His values. Nothing can move you out of God's presence, unless you give it permission to do so by your choices. Therefore, to be established in the peace of God, make the choice to "set your mind" on what God speaks to you in His Word.

What keeps us from experiencing the peace of God?

- Impatience. We step away from peace when we are unwilling to "wait on God" for His guidance, when we are faced with stressful situations.
- When we allow our feelings to rule over our better judgment, we tend to make impulsive decisions rather than being led by God's wisdom.
- Unrealistic expectations. Where do our expectations lie? Do we place our hopes and expectations in people, or do we trust God to fulfill the desires of our heart?
- Fear. Are we governed by our fears, which limit who we really are? Fear immobilizes us, preventing us from making positive changes that lead to peace.
- Regrets. Do we allow our perceived limitations to hold us back from moving forward? God never gives up on us! No excuse justifies staying in a place of hopelessness.
- Self pity. Living in this state is a big black hole of despair, leading to depression and resignation. God's peace cannot exist in us while we focus on our hopeless state. There is always hope when we turn to God for help.

Now let's look at how we can enter the peace of God, regardless of our circumstances.

- Change your focus! Turn to Jesus in your thoughts. Meditate on the Promises of God for you in Scripture. When you feel overwhelmed and don't know what to do, say the following prayer: *"Jesus, thank you that you are with me in this trial, that you are in front of me leading the way, and also behind me to cover and protect me as I choose to believe You, over and above these difficult circumstances."* We are always strengthened in our spirit as we declare our love for God, which brings peace into our soul.

- Realize you are not alone! God is with you, even when you don't feel His presence. The more you choose God's Way over your fears, the greater revelation you will experience of His presence within you.
- Be aware that God is always in control of our life. He allows us to go through testing times to show us how much we need Him. Our trials reveal what truly lies buried in our heart. In Exodus, the Israelites experienced great hardship in the wilderness, which caused them to complain and grumble. How faithful are we to follow God's wisdom and leading during the difficult seasons of our life, maintaining a positive attitude and trusting in Him?
- Adjust your expectations to depend upon God rather than people.
- Choose to do what you can to change your circumstances, and release what you cannot do to God.
- Be aware that everything you go through will be used by God to ultimately bless you, and bring victory in your life, meaning you will overcome all adversity as you trust in and depend upon God.

To summarize, here are some keys to help you remain in the peace of God:

- Don't take on the issues of others as your personal responsibility. By all means pray and help them in any way you can, but do not carry their burdens on your own shoulders (meaning in your soul).
- Consciously step aside from turmoil and conflict, by choosing to focus on how God leads you towards His peace.
- Realize God is "always in control." Ask Him what it is you need to learn in this present circumstance you are facing.
- Be honest about your part in a challenging situation, and repent if you are led to do so.
- Take a stand against the spirit of fear that causes you to feel defeated. You have nothing to fear when you choose God's Way.

- Don't fall into the trap of defending yourself against the perceived judgments of people who may be causing conflict in your life. Pray for them, and choose to let go of any offenses towards them. Release them to God in love and forgiveness. Bless them in any way God leads you to do so.
- Realize Jesus Christ paid the full price for you by taking EVERY trial you are experiencing upon Himself. You do not need to carry what He already sacrificed for you, so that you may live in peace and freedom.
- Come into agreement with the truth that you are already established as God's chosen one. This is who you really are. You are not a victim.
- Carry this truth in your heart as you navigate through all of life's challenges.
- *Become* peace by how you see yourself, and by the choices you make to stand on the Rock of Christ. This is how you can abide in eternal peace through all the storms life brings your way.

Secrets of the Hiding Place

When we choose God's love, we choose His peace, because that is who God is.

You are a masterpiece of Creation; don't waste your God-given gifts!

What do we need to give up in order to abide in God's peace?

- We need to relinquish our own need to protect our ego, by justifying our negative choices.
- We have to surrender our need to be 'right' in the eyes of others.
- We need to become humble to make room for God in our heart. Why? Because as long as our ego remains in control, we are not giving God permission to act on our behalf.
- Simplify your life by letting go of unnecessary distractions that steal your peace.
- Do not allow pride to get in the way of being your authentic self.

Find inner peace by choosing to live the destiny God created for you!

Scripture: Psalm 37:23-24 (NLT)

"The steps of the godly are directed by the Lord. He delights in every detail of their lives. Though they stumble, they will not fall, for the Lord holds them by the hand."

Do you believe you were born with a destiny and a special purpose?

There is undeniable evidence that our Universe was created perfectly by divine order. Science reveals mathematical proof that the earth, stars and planets hold their position according to divine design. Why would human beings be an exception to such perfect order? Some of us discover our innate purpose early in life. Others spend a lifetime seeking reasons to justify their existence. We could ask the question: Am I attuned to the world's values, or to God? Children intuitively sense their real value and natural gifts. A parent's role is to recognize these gifts and guide their children towards developing them. Within each of us is a blueprint to guide us to our destiny. This blueprint, which is unique in every person, could be likened to a navigation instrument designed to keep us "on course," if we are attuned to it. The problem is, we become distracted by the noise and busyness of our outer environment that takes us off course. We need to attune ourselves to listen to our inner compass. This does not occur naturally in our Western civilization. I wrote earlier about Mayan children who are protected from being exposed to so-called civilized values, allowing them to grow up in a natural environment that enables them to remain innocent and pure in heart. The challenge for people raised in our Western culture is to re-connect to our true self, the child within us, with untouched potential to be all God created us to be. We need to learn how to 'turn off' the noise around us and tune in to our inner self, the spirit within us. How do we do this? We make choices to simplify our life. How? We learn to think as a child again.

How do we do this?

- We begin by changing our thought life to establish a new way of thinking.
- We make different choices in our priorities, eliminating whatever complicates our life.
- We stop 'excessive reasoning' which causes confusion in our thoughts.
- We refuse to worry about those things we have no control over.
- We consciously seek to enter into our "hiding place in God," to rest our mind in quiet places, thus separating ourselves from conflict and confusion. We can do this in our imagination, as we visualize ourselves entering into God's presence. Form a picture in your mind of a serene setting, like a lagoon set in a forest where you can contemplate in peace. When you enter quietness, God can speak to your spirit and give you rest.
- Turn off the television, go for walks in Nature, study Scripture, listen to beautiful music, spend time observing children at play, pray, meditate, read inspirational books, slow down by getting off the treadmill of constant activity. If you make a habit of choosing quietness every now and then, you will be re-charged to keep connected to the child within you. This will enable God to direct your steps and guide you to fulfill your God-given destiny.
- Choose peace over your own efforts and emotional needs. When you are in peace, everything else in your life flows more evenly.
- Do not allow your happiness to be conditional upon the circumstances in your life.
- Contentment is born out of acceptance.

It is Christ in us who is our hope and source of peace!

When we connect with the love of God and know He is enough for us, peace reigns in our soul. Living from this revelation protects us from the fear of loss, bringing freedom to live fully in the moment. When confronted with challenges, pray to God to help you stay in peace rather than give in to fear. When we are peaceful, we know exactly what we need to do, because we are not confused by our fluctuating emotions. The peace of God gives us supernatural power to help us confront problems with wisdom. When we live in a godly way, our life will reflect the character of God. God IS love, therefore love is always God's motivation and purpose for us. When we are motivated by love, the root of God's power is established in our heart, and in how we live.

Scripture: Ephesians 3:17-18 (NLT)

"I pray that Christ will be more and more at home in your hearts as you trust in Him. May your roots go down deep into the soil of God's marvelous love. And may you have the power to understand, as all God's people should, how wide, how long, how high and how deep His love really is."

Secrets of the Hiding Place

Your brain is your instrument. Your thoughts are the music. God is your conductor.

Lift darkness by offering praise and thanksgiving to God.

REFLECTIONS

- How do we win the war between chaos and peace in our mind?

- What is true peace, and what are its lasting benefits?

- Write down some of the keys to experiencing peace in your life.

- What do we need to change within us in order to experience God's peace?

- Do you believe you were born with a destiny and a special purpose?

- If you believe this, list some of the steps laid out in this chapter to help you fulfill your destiny.

- What may be preventing you from walking the path God has chosen for you?

- Can you identify what the blocks may be? Write them down in detail.

- Now, ask yourself what you need to change in your heart and mind to remove these blocks.

- Picture yourself living the life God has revealed to you, without any impediments holding you back.

- Look for Scriptures of God's promises for you, and claim them into your heart and mind. Quote them aloud each day over yourself.

Chapter Twelve

WORSHIPING GOD

WORSHIP IS THE POSITION OF OUR HEART TURNED TOWARDS GOD

Why worship God?

Scripture: John 4:23-24 (NLT)

"The time is coming and is already here when true worshipers will worship the Father in spirit and in truth. The Father is looking for anyone who will worship Him that way. For God is Spirit, so those who worship Him must worship in spirit and truth."

*K*ing David knew he could not live without God's protection. Many of the Psalms he wrote leave no doubt he depended upon God constantly to keep him safe from his adversaries. Most of the years he reigned as King were spent fighting against his enemies. David knew the pain of betrayal, deep loneliness, abandonment and rejection, YET, he also knew whom to turn to for help in all his troubles. David was a servant to the Almighty God, whom he worshiped throughout the devastating circumstances he faced daily. Why do I refer to him in writing about the importance of worshiping God? Because King David experienced pain just as we do. He serves as an example of how to live our lives successfully, and how to face disaster with a kingly mindset. As followers of Jesus Christ, we also carry the banner of kingship to live our lives knowing who we truly are as children of God. We are carriers of God's Holy Spirit, meaning we have a royal heritage, just as King David did.

What does this mean to us?

We are born to rule over darkness (principalities of earth) by taking a stand against evil. We cannot compromise what we stand for as emissaries of God's kingdom values.

How do we take a stand for Truth?

First of all, we step into who God created us to be. We do this by reading Scriptures that teach us about our God-given identity, and by studying the lives of people like King David.

- We get to know the nature of God by studying the many names given to Him, and what they represent (refer to Chapter Eight in this book).
- We turn to God in every aspect of our life, placing His values over our own as we deal with challenges.
- We worship God in our heart. As we do this we step into God's value system, joining our spirit with His Spirit.
- Worshiping God in our heart means we are choosing to come under the banner (covering) of His love, protection and promises. In other words, we are agreeing to covenant with God, to be one with Him in how we live our life.

In legal terms, covenant means an agreement between two parties that is legally binding. When we covenant with God to enter into relationship with Him through His Son Jesus, we place ourselves in position to receive all the blessings He offers us, including His amazing gift of grace.

How does God's grace bless us?

- Grace is God's unmerited favour in our life
- Grace is a gift we cannot earn
- Grace is hope eternal
- Grace is peace beyond human understanding
- Grace is divine wisdom to guide us
- Grace is joy in the midst of turmoil
- Grace is Godly protection against evil
- Grace is supernatural strength and courage to go through our valleys
- Grace is all the fruits of the Spirit promised by God
- Grace is answered prayers
- Grace is rest and safety in life's storms

Secret of the Hiding Place

Grace is the power of God's Holy Spirit manifested in our life.

Why is it important to worship God?

What or whom we worship reveals what we value most highly, meaning, what we think about, and where we focus most of our time and attention, becomes our lifestyle and identity.

What we focus on eventually forms our character!

Our character becomes who we believe we are in our core values, and from our core values, we make choices that steer us in the direction our life takes us. Therefore, our life becomes a reflection of who or what we hold most dear, and who or what we worship. There is no compromise in God's kingdom values. We cannot barter our way into favour and blessings from God, who sees the motives of our heart. The irony is, when we choose God's Way, doors of grace open for us to enter into a lifestyle far above anything our physical world can give us. We enter into the spiritual realm of grace, where even mundane events in our life take on a quality of exquisite beauty, highlighting God's eternal values like prisms of heavenly light. In other words, we enter His world of unconditional love, peace, rest, and prophetic insight, to see the deeper meanings and purposes behind what we go through in the varied experiences of our human existence.

Secrets of the Hiding Place

Worshiping brings us into God's holiness.

Worship is how we interact with the Lord and connect with His heart.

What does being holy mean?

Holiness is a hunger in our heart and mind to connect with Truth. It is *not* a state of perfection where we do not make mistakes. Our journey towards the state of holiness is the process of purification of our human-self, until we become a pure vessel worthy of carrying God's glory. This is how God prepares us to fulfill His purposes for us on earth. When our character is refined enough to place God ahead of our own ego, He will shine His glory through us to bless others. The transformation that takes place is in our heart, so that we *want* to serve God in any way He directs us. This is the process of transforming us from our old ego-self, to become who we were created to be, a blessing to others.

Jesus Christ lived a life of holiness where His motivation was to please God, to do the will of His Father in Heaven. The road to holiness does not guarantee us happiness (as we understand happiness by worldly values), or the avoidance of pain, because in Scripture we are taught to "go through our valleys" rather than avoid them. Our society has become a lifestyle of avoiding pain at all costs, to find quick fixes to our problems. We look for ways to escape the consequences of our actions, to hide from facing truth that may hurt our ego. We have become masters of avoiding pain by depending on drugs, or other forms of distractions to bury our deepest emotions, rather than face reality. Do not fear pain, for it has its purpose. Pain reveals the need to 'push through' our trials, because there are always lessons to be learned in them. We gain strength by not giving up. Grit and determination are the tools of success needed during our trials and losses. We win by our determination to never quit. God does the rest!

What is true holiness and what does it look like in our life?

- Holiness is the state of knowing you are in the place God created you for, to follow your God-given destiny. It is your core belief that you were born for a divine purpose.
- Holiness is an inner awareness rather than outward circumstances.
- Holiness is the undeniable conviction of your self-worth as God sees you, even when people in your life may not recognize or value who you really are.
- Holiness is grounded in godly principles rather than temporary values.
- Holiness is letting go of control of people or circumstances you cannot change.
- Holiness is choosing simplicity over confusion.
- Holiness is being ruled by wisdom rather than your emotions.
- Holiness is seeking God's will in all things.
- Holiness is being willing to be misjudged by people when you take a stand for what you believe.
- Holiness is choosing to please God rather than people.
- Holiness is being true to your deep inner convictions.
- Holiness is the act of trusting God rather than your fears.
- Holiness is peace in your heart and soul.
- Holiness is self-control and discipline.
- Holiness is treating everyone with value.

When we worship God, we are declaring with our mind, heart and emotions that everything we are, including our weaknesses, belong to Him.

Secret of the Hiding Place

As you radiate love to others, God's light within you increases in power to illuminate the path of Truth for them to follow.

196

REDEEMING GRACE

God's grace is a gift, given freely, often to those who seem unworthy.

The power of grace cannot be explained, for it goes against man's reasoning mind.

Grace transforms our broken hearts to look up high at the face of God.

Grace reaches in to places dark, stirring new life and shining bright

into souls succumbed to the night, bringing hope with dawn's new light.

The touch of grace is a touch from God unfurled from heaven to bless our lives,

turning us from worldly cares to face His Son who casts out fear.

God's grace does not discriminate as people do in the human race.

He sees each one as complete and whole; His perfect love covers the world.

And once His grace touches us, we become a new creature, redeemed at last

to live in God's kingdom of love and peace, fully free because of His grace.

REFLECTIONS

- Why do we need to worship God?

- How do we take a stand for God's Truths in our life?

- Describe what Scripture means to "covenant" with God?

- Describe what grace means to you.

- How does God's grace bless us?

- What does it mean to be 'holy?'

- What would true holiness look like in your life?

- How does worshiping God bring closer intimacy with Him?

Chapter Thirteen

THE POWER OF THANKFULNESS

Scripture: 1 Thessalonians 5:18 (Amplified Bible)

"Thank (God) in everything (no matter what the circumstances may be, be thankful and give thanks), for this is the will of God for you (who are) in Christ Jesus (the Revealer and Mediator of that will)."

Saint Paul wrote about thanksgiving as he experienced persecution, pain and suffering in prison. He understood that a thankful heart is a spiritual sword, which wields God's justice in unjust circumstances. Thanksgiving is a tool to overcome all strategies of evil we may encounter in our lives. It is not God's will for us to suffer. Suffering is the result of a fallen world where darkness pervades in so many ways. Our responsibility, as believers in God, is to focus on His good will for us with our faith, regardless of what our circumstances look like. This is how our faith grows, where we become increasingly mature in our journey through life. Our challenge is to trust God, and believe He is in control while we 'go through' the trials that face us. During the times we are tempted to give into hopelessness, we must take a stand and declare: *"God is bigger than what I am going through. Thank you Lord for Your will prevailing in this situation. I belong to You, and believe You will bring good from what*

I am experiencing." The battle is the Lord's! **(Romans 12:21 - NIV)** **"Do not be overcome by evil, but overcome evil with good."**

A grateful heart is a contented heart

We tend to take so much for granted until it is taken from us. I know God is teaching me this lesson in what I am presently experiencing in my life. Since I was a very young child, I have loved to take long walks in Nature. When I lived in the Outback of Australia up to six years of age, I explored the vast bush lands that stretched as far as one could see behind our little town. I discovered trails and hidden rock caves that I believed, in my young imagination, to be homes of creatures living in the bush. As I grew older, when we lived in Melbourne, I would walk for hours to explore places I had never been, wondering what new discoveries lay beyond the next hill. During the years I was being sexually abused by my father, walking became my escape from feeling trapped and hopeless; this was the only way I knew how to cleanse my soul of the emotional pain in my heart. I share this with you to explain what it feels like to have something precious taken away.

Recently I was injured, which left me with severe sciatic pain in my lower back, preventing me from walking more than a few steps. I have been grieving the loss of something I had relied on and taken for granted most of my life. I know God has not abandoned me in this painful journey, and that there is a lesson for me to learn as I lean on Him to bring me through this valley. In the five months since this injury occurred, I have experienced ongoing pain beyond anything I could have imagined. I have been faced with two choices. Either I give in and give up, falling into unbelief that God will not heal me, or, I choose to believe God is in control, that He is my Healer and that I need to trust Him in this process, and in His timing. I have chosen to believe God, not my fears or feelings. I am focusing on writing this book to keep my heart and mind attuned to God's will for me. There have been times I felt like giving up, yet I know I must not do this. I choose to believe God and rest in His promises for me, that I will be made whole and be able to take long walks in Nature again without pain. I have chosen to live with a grateful heart for all the wonderful things God has done, and what He will continue to do for me, and for all the people I love and care about.

Scripture: 2 Corinthians 4:15 (Amplified Bible)

"For all (these) things (taking place) for your sake, so that the more grace (divine favour and spiritual blessing) extends to more and more people and multiplies through the many, the more thanksgiving may increase to the glory of God."

I am encouraged by Corrie ten Boom's story in her book, The Hiding Place, her autobiography about the years she spent in a concentration camp during World War 11. Her message is profound, about how she and her sister Betsie coped with the atrocities they endured in this camp. Their faith in Jesus Christ enabled them to endure what most of us would consider impossible conditions. The building they slept in was riddled with lice that bit them as they slept, causing pain and great discomfort. Corrie wrote about how difficult it was to deal with this, and how her sister Betsie looked upon the lice as a blessing from God. Why? Because the prison guards would never enter this building, knowing they would be bitten by the lice. This enabled those living there to hold prayer and worship meetings, and to commune with God freely without being caught and punished. The lesson here is; there is always something we can be grateful for if we open our heart to see this truth. By living in gratitude, we allow God to move into our difficult circumstances to do His will in and through us.

Thankfulness is a godly principle

In **1st Thessalonians 5:18** where we are instructed to give thanks in all our circumstances, this does not make sense from our worldly perspective. How can we do this while we are experiencing loss and pain? It helps to understand God's law of "moving in the opposite spirit." Let me explain what I believe this means.

- We give power, through our thoughts and emotions, to whatever we focus on.

- Our feelings follow our thoughts, therefore, whatever direction our thoughts take us adds power to feed our emotions, whether positive or negative.
- We have been given free will to make our own choices.
- Scripture is our guide from God to teach us His godly principles to make wise choices, according to His kingdom values. The more we understand God's perspective in our trials, the wiser our choices will be.
- We are not victims of our circumstances, unless we believe this lie.
- The key to changing our negative, harmful circumstances is to have a heart revelation of who we truly are in God's sight.
- We have been given keys from Heaven, to open new doors that lead to victory over our problems, and also to shut doors that lead us to failure.
- The power to change lives within us. Holy Spirit is our teacher, our guide, our correction when we err, our friend and lover of our soul. As we choose to focus on God's leading in every aspect of our life, we become 'overcomers' by our choices to follow God's Way in our trials.
- As we make conscious choices to "think as God thinks," by applying Scriptural principles in our thoughts and actions, we 'open the door' for the power of God to be activated in our life. We 'feed' our soul with God's promises freely given to us, by agreeing with them. God will do the rest!
- As we 'rest' in God's promises for us, we are fed Living Waters from Him to sustain us through our difficult seasons of life. This is how we are able to move in the opposite direction of our circumstances. We do this from a position of resting in God, and trusting His Word, which promises to bring us to victory.
- We are not alone!
- Live with thankfulness in your heart and press in to God's presence.
- The key is to truly believe His Word, and stand on the Rock of Christ as you face life's storms. Commit to continue believing Him through all your difficulties. Maintain a position of faith in your heart, and doors will open to bring you into the atmosphere

of Heaven, where you will experience the peace of God, whatever is occurring in your life.

Secret of the Hiding Place

Whatever you do not value, you eventually lose. Be fully engaged in this moment and discover its value!

Exercise to help you come into alignment with how God sees you

Write down all the things you can be thankful for from your past, and in the present time. When you are experiencing trials that seem overwhelming to you right now, it helps to re-focus your mind on the many blessings that have already happened, and also those that are presently taking place in your life. This will help you to face the future with more confidence, knowing God will not forget you in your present need. It takes determination to get our mind off what is occurring at this moment, yet as we obey God, (by believing He hears our prayers and will bring us through our trials), we step into the realm of breakthroughs and victories available to all His children. As I look back over my life, I realize that all those circumstances I feared would never end, always did end. Nothing lasts forever and life moves on, no matter how bad it seems while we are going through it. There is always hope when we choose God over everything else.

What gives your life purpose and meaning?

If you knew your life span was close to drawing to an end, would you be concerned about all the minor frustrations that have caused you to lose your peace in the last few days or weeks? I suspect you would focus on those things you are deeply thankful for, that you may have taken for granted in the past (while trying to keep up with the rush and busyness of life). What gives life beauty and meaning? Our Western society has lost its sense of enchantment, and the value of simplicity, while pursuing what is considered success. I am old enough to remember when life moved at a much slower pace, when we had time to attend to our responsibilities and chores without feeling pressured and stressed. Today I watch people focusing on texting as they are supposedly taking a break from work to relax over a coffee; their attention appears to be geared to what others are expecting from them as they answer whatever has been texted to them on their iphone. I see around me souls who are hungry for beauty and love, but do not know how to reach this place. I get the impression many people have lost touch with innocence and the sweetness of life.

What captures your attention?

This may be a good question to ask yourself. I know I need to remind myself often of what is really important to me, so that I can keep in touch with what is real and meaningful each and every day of my life.

Secret of the Hiding Place

Thankfulness opens the door to Heavenly blessings.

THANKFULNESS

I give God thanks for who I am, an integral part of His Holy plan

to be an expression of His great love, like falling rain from Heaven above.

And as I face life's challenges, my love for Him will never cease

because I know He's here with me, through all my trials to eternity;

they are just a moment in time, like moving waters rushing by.

I choose to lift my countenance and spend my time in God's presence,

to celebrate the gift of life that brought me here from the moment of birth.

Each precious day that I have lived brings thankfulness into my heart,

as I reflect on all the ways God carried me through my trials and joys.

So as I rest in blessed peace, I thank You Lord for choosing me

to worship You in how I live, until I reach my journey's end.

REFLECTIONS

- Why does God instruct us to "give thanks in everything?" (1st Thessalonians 5:18).

- I suggest you read the book THE HIDING PLACE by Corrie ten Boom (see reference on last page) to help you understand why a thankful heart enriches your life.

- Describe how thankfulness is a godly principle.

- Do the exercise in this chapter to clarify the value of living in thankfulness.

- Make a list of everything in your life that you are grateful for, and make a point of thanking God for the small blessings in each day.

- Write in your journal what is really important to you, what captures your attention to stir new hope in your heart, and give meaning to your life.

Chapter Fourteen

AN INVITATION TO YOU

Scripture: Romans 8:31-32 (NLT)

"If God is for us, who can ever be against us? Since God did not spare even His own Son but gave Him up for us all, won't God, who gave us Christ, also give us everything else?"

INVITATION

You are invited to join the Lord at His Banquet Table to partake of His heartfelt blessings from Heaven, to receive His peace, comfort, physical and emotional healing and ever-lasting life. You are an heir, chosen to receive God's inheritance because you are "family," born into His bloodline with all the privileges due from His heavenly kingdom. Please respond rsvp to confirm whether you accept God's invitation, by saying the following prayer:

"Lord, I would be honoured to join you at Your Banquet Table to partake in all the gifts you have offered me. I come to Your Table with an open heart filled with thankfulness as your son/daughter, to receive with gratitude my Royal heritage in Your kingdom.

Signed: (...)

Preparing for the Royal Feast

*W*hat preparations are required to get ready for a Royal celebration? Think of yourself as a bride being prepared for marriage to your King. Remember, as believers we are all called the Bride of Christ. In Scripture, Queen Esther was chosen to marry the King because of her open heart, her inner and outer beauty, as well as her courage and desire to serve her people. She went through a year of rituals and pampering before her marriage to the King. What do we need to do to prepare ourselves for our King? This principle applies to everyone invited, both men and women in His kingdom.

Important keys to remember:

- Recognition of the significance of being chosen to join our Lord to partake in everything He offers us.
- Humility in our spirit to receive what Father God has chosen to give us.
- A pure heart open to placing God first, over and above everything else in our life.
- Courage to commit to what God has chosen for us, to follow our destiny.
- Childlike trust to believe who we are in Him.
- Forgiveness to all who have hurt or abused us in our past.
- The decision to refuse to hold any offenses towards anyone.
- A hunger in our heart to serve others and bless them as God leads us.
- Choosing love over protecting our pride.

How do we fulfill the above requirements?

We commit to listening to Holy Spirit's directions within us, and to obey His leading, one step at a time. As we surrender our old ways, with the willingness to conform to where God is leading us, we enable Holy Spirit to change us in this journey of being transformed into Christ's image. We will not have victory if we strive in our own strength to become who God created us to be. Surrender is the key! When our peace is threatened by disturbing situations or people in our life (where we feel upset, angry or defensive, and are tempted to react negatively), turn to God in your spirit and say the following prayer quietly to your-self: **(Psalm 51:10 - NLT) "Create in me a clean heart, O God. Renew a right spirit in me."** You will be amazed at how instanta-neously your mood lifts and your feelings of peace are restored. When this happens, I instantly thank God for answering my prayer for help.

What do we need to surrender?

- Our need to be right in our own eyes and the opinions of others.
- Our need to be 'in control,' rather than submitting ourselves to serving the needs of people whom God places in our path.
- Our desire to serve our emotional needs above what Holy Spirit is leading us to do (even when this requires sacrifices from us).
- Protecting our ego by justifying a rebellious attitude towards people and God.
- Excessive habits that lead to an unbalanced lifestyle.
- The need to hide old shame and guilt.

What blessings do we receive when we choose to follow God's will in our life?

- We give God permission to heal our heart and soul from old wounds, so that He can fully restore and renew us **(Isaiah 61:4).**
- We carry His anointing power that enables us to become instru-ments of peace, and a blessing upon earth.
- We are given authority by God to decree His truths into peo-ple's lives.
- Our lives are fulfilled as we grow in wisdom and revelation, to reflect God's kingdom values "on earth as it is in heaven."
- God's peace becomes our refuge in times of trouble, protecting us from all evil **(Psalm 91).**
- We are set free from the spirit of fear and worry, as we trust God rather than our feelings.

In this journey of surrendering ourselves to God's will, this does not mean we are deprived of the good things available to us. God provided the many blessings in this world for our pleasure. Our responsibility is to keep our heart pure by not allowing our emotions to rule us, where we can become enslaved by our appetites. We cannot serve two masters at the same time. We are given the choice to serve ourselves, or God. The irony is, as we give ourselves away by serving others, we discover our true self. This is how we connect to the heart of God, by aligning ourselves with His divine purposes for our life. Whatever we sacrifice in this process diminishes in value, as we mature into who God created us to become.

The longings in our heart

Have you ever stopped to analyze what drives you to pursue the longings in your heart? From early childhood dreams are placed deep in our soul that stir up passion within us to fulfill them. These dreams are unique to each person, the personal DNA in our heart that calls us to fulfill who we were created to become. I believe this is a gift from God stamped on our soul by His love and approval of us, a Promissory Note from heaven for us. Children need spiritual mentors who understand God's divine plans for them, to help guide them into their unique destinies. The most profound influences in children's lives come by way of living examples of Kingdom principles, from the people they grow up with. If we grow up not receiving godly guidance, the dreams and longings in our heart often get buried as we mature, and take on the responsibilities of life. However, it is never too late to re-awaken them, and get in touch with dreams from our youth that have been set aside.

A New Beginning!

Wherever you may be in your journey, God knows the longings in your heart. Allow Him to enter this void within you that only He can fill. He has a new beginning for you! Believe this truth! I am in my 75th year and I can testify that God reveals Himself in amazing ways, whatever age we are. There are unlimited opportunities waiting to be discovered; live with the expectation you will learn something new every day. We must never give up our dreams, for they are the fire of hope burning in our heart to keep us moving forward. When we stop dreaming, we stop living in the true sense of what living means.

How does God reveal Himself to us? To explain this question I will share how God has revealed Himself to me.

I wrote earlier about an injury to my back where I experienced months of excruciating sciatic pain that prevented me from being able to walk, and many nights, from sleeping. I have been through a great deal of physical and emotional pain in my life, yet nothing prepared me for this. It felt as though a red-hot burning drill was pushing into my tailbone, pressing on the sciatic nerve, which radiated pain into my buttocks and down my legs to the feet. The constant high-level nerve pain wore me out, stealing my peace and consuming my energy. During the long evenings when I was unable to sleep, I sat at my computer to push through the pain by focusing on writing this book. At times I felt as though I was fighting for my very existence, just to survive and get through each moment. It was in this place I surrendered every part of my life and myself to Jesus. If He didn't bring me through this battle, I knew I could not do it for myself. I often read aloud the Psalms of King David and could so relate to when he felt alone and discouraged, yet at the same time, I was encouraged by his faith as he declared that God always brought him through his trials and testing times.

God knows us intimately, our hidden pain, disappointments, the abuse we may have experienced, any rejection we received, and all our buried dreams that have not been fulfilled. My personal experience in going through this testing time has revealed some profound truths that I will share with you now. The following thoughts were written in my journal during a recent trip to Punta Cana in the Dominican Republic, where I spent two weeks with my daughter, son-in-law and their five children.

Journal writings - November, 2014

I am writing in my journal on the balcony of our room overlooking the Atlantic Ocean. I woke up this morning with the dawn around 6 am, while the girls were still sleeping. The scene in front of me is like a picture-postcard. The sky is dotted with puffs of cotton candy clouds that are reflected on the azure blue water, where waves are breaking against reefs about a mile from shore. Gentle breezes caress the palm trees that line the many pathways spread along miles of soft white sand. The ocean water is warm, and each morning I spend an hour or more swimming there to soak up its healing effects. This trip is a gift from God to me, for I am spending two weeks here with my precious family. This holiday has come at the right time, because I am now able to get around with a cane, and the pain level has diminished. I believe that after two weeks of gentle exercise in the ocean, I won't even need the cane any more. In this process of healing, I have experienced God's presence at a much deeper level than ever before in my soul. I would never have chosen to go through the terrible pain of the past seven months, yet in all of that, I have been released to enter into what I could call the "holy of holies," where whatever was blocking me from being this close to God, has been removed. I wasn't consciously aware of any blocks, however, I believe God reveals hidden pain deep in our soul in degrees. We could not handle the trauma of all our pain being released at one time. At the height of my pain, I prayed from the very core of my being. I declared out loud in my prayers to God that "every cell of my body, every breath, every heartbeat, every longing in my heart, every regret I held from the past, every offense or unforgiveness I still held onto, belonged to Him." Spiritually speaking, I lay myself down at the altar of God. I surrendered all of myself to Him and declared that I belong completely to Him. There was a cleansing taking place deep within my soul, as I humbled myself and declared I needed Jesus like I needed breath to live. The following Scripture describes what it means to hunger for God's presence.

Scripture: Psalm 42:1 (NLT)

"As the deer pants for streams of water, so I long for You O God. I thirst for God, the living God. When can I come and stand before Him?"

What really transpired in surrendering my all to God?

What took place was a "divine exchange" where I gave all of myself to receive all of God! In surrendering to His will during my struggles, weakness and pain, He revealed Himself to me on a much deeper level than I had experienced previously. The following are some of the truths God revealed to me through my recent trials. As you reflect on them, can you relate to some of these revelations in your own life?

- I now understand how vulnerable I am to outside influences, like pain and circumstances beyond my control.
- I have been humbled in my humanity, realizing life is a gift that should never be taken for granted.
- God is much bigger than me!
- I realize that believing I have control of my life outside of God's domain is an illusion.
- I know I belong to a much bigger plan and purpose in my life, that what I used to consider important really doesn't matter.
- The longings in my heart are dreams God planted in me, to fulfill what He created for me.
- I am divinely connected to all people, as part of God's universal design for humanity.
- Selfishness separates me from God.
- My purpose as a human being is to align myself with God.
- Surrender is not a bad word! As I surrender to God's will and kingdom values, I discover who I really am.
- My true value is who I am in God, not in how others see me.
- Striving to fulfill my own needs, rather than depending on God, will wear me out.
- As I depend on God to guide me, His strength will sustain me in my own weaknesses.
- My true identity and value as a human being were chosen by God, even before my birth.
- I have nothing to fear as I rest, abide and trust in God. He will never fail me.
- God's peace in my heart is the greatest of all gifts.
- My life is in His hands. Period!

Secret of the Hiding Place

God reveals Himself through us as we choose to live according to His heavenly kingdom values. Ask Holy Spirit to guide you in this journey. He always shows up!

I share these revelations with you to use my life as a testimony of how precious life is. The most awesome revelation for me has been how God reveals Himself in our times of greatest weakness, when we come to the point where we are ready to admit we truly need Him, and are willing to give the reins of our life to Him. This may sound contradictory to what I wrote in earlier chapters about choosing the quality of our life through the thoughts we think. To clarify this point, we are given free will to choose our way or God's Way, and by choosing to surrender to God by following kingdom principles, we align ourselves with His divine plans for us. It is in this place we receive His promises and blessings in our life. The longing in my heart is to encourage you to trust God, especially when you experience feelings of hopelessness and discouragement as you face your own trials. He is waiting for you to run to Papa, to open your heart and ask for His help. You were chosen and created by Him for a definite purpose, and He will never let you down. He is waiting with open arms to embrace you as you turn to Him and ask for help, in whatever circumstances you are facing.

Scripture: James 4:10 (NLT)

"When you bow down before the Lord and admit your dependence on him, he will lift you up and give you honour."

Please accept the Lord's invitation to join Him at His Banquet Table, to partake of His grace, unconditional love, peace and all the gifts available to you as His child.

REFLECTIONS

- Are you ready to respond to the Lord's invitation to join Him at His Banquet Table?

- What are some of the requirements in preparing for this Royal occasion, and how do we fulfill them in our life?

- What part does surrendering to God's will play in these preparations?

- Describe some of the blessings we receive when we surrender to God's Way.

- What are some of the unfulfilled longings in your heart?

- How can you re-awaken these dreams and make them a reality in your life now?

- Journal what you believe your life would look like if you were to surrender yourself to God.

- Are there some things you are holding back from God? What are they?

- If you are holding anything back, why are you having difficulty in trusting God to take care of you? Be honest with your answers, and ask Holy Spirit to help you release to God anything separating you from close intimacy with Him.

- Journal the ways God has revealed Himself to you.

Chapter Fifteen

HOLY SPIRIT REVEALED

Who is Holy Spirit?

*H*oly Spirit is the Person of God. This means He is everything God is in Spirit. When we ask Jesus Christ into our life, Holy Spirit enters our spirit to live within us. From that moment on, He resides in our being. We become a 'home' to Him. This means God Himself is living in us!!! We have now become the recipient of *all* that God is; we carry His DNA within us to transform us into His image during our lifespan on earth. God's DNA becomes our DNA in this process of transformation **(2 Corinthians 5:17) "Those who become Christians become new persons. They are not the same anymore, for the old life is gone. A new life has begun!"** We are connected to God's vine **(John 15:5) "Yes, I am the vine; you are the branches. Those who remain in Me and I in them, will produce much fruit. For apart from Me you can do nothing."**

When we are connected to God's vine, we become recipients of everything He has to give us.

Our role is to 'listen' and follow the leading of Holy Spirit as He guides us through our human journey. Holy Spirit is depicted as a dove in Scripture. Why is this? Doves are sensitive, gentle creatures that fly away from noise and disturbances, therefore, when we are quiet and reflective, we are more likely to connect with Holy Spirit in us. As long as we allow busyness to distract our attention, we will 'grieve' the Holy Spirit **(Ephesians 4:30).** This is why I write about entering into God's "hiding place" to be able to hear what Holy Spirit is communicating to us. This is a beautiful place to live in our heart and soul. The more we seek His presence, the hungrier we become for more of Him. Eventually, this way of living becomes a lifestyle, where we automatically commune with God's Holy Spirit for ALL our needs.

How do we align ourselves with Holy Spirit's leading? We acknowledge Him in our heart and include Him in our thoughts and life. We "give permission" to Holy Spirit to rule our life. We surrender our old nature, to come under the dominion and authority of God's guidance, through His Holy Spirit. We make the choice to turn away from our old ways (our identity before Christ entered our heart). How do we do this? We ask Holy Spirit to renew our mind according to the Word of God in Scripture, and to help us release all those things we relied on previously to cope with our challenges. I call these 'coping strategies' we use to deal with life when we are fearful. They become our 'props' that hold us up when we are faced with situations that appear to be beyond our control.

Let's identify some of these props:

- Addictions of any kind – food, drugs, alcoholism, excessive negative behaviors and uncontrolled habits that hurt us.
- Wearing 'masks' to avoid dealing with truth.
- Needing approval from others to give us value.
- Inability to face the consequences of our actions.
- Unresolved anger.
- Blaming others for our own problems.
- Self-pity.
- Judging others to elevate our self-importance.
- Denial of our own shortcomings.
- Fears of any kind.

Now let's look at some of the blessings we receive when we trust Holy Spirit:

- God's presence is always with us.

- We are divinely connected to God's love, power and protection at all times.
- We experience peace beyond human understanding **(Philippians 4:7).**
- We have our "Helper" to guide and direct us in all our human needs.
- Holy Spirit is our "Teacher" who reveals the nature of God to us.
- Holy Spirit knows our needs even before we ask for help.
- Holy Spirit is our "Comforter" in times of sadness, trouble and grief.
- He is the Lover of our soul. He knows our deepest needs as we live our human journey.
- Holy Spirit will never leave nor forsake us. He is our trusted friend at all times.

How do we connect with Holy Spirit?

- We recognize Who He is, the living Spirit of God.
- We surrender all that we are, to live under God's authority through His Holy Spirit within us.
- We give all honour and glory to Him.
- We choose to trust Him over and above our old ways of coping with life.
- We spend time meditating on God's Word, and ask Holy Spirit to reveal His truths in Scripture.
- We place God first in our priorities, turning first to Him before anything or anyone else.
- We communicate with Holy Spirit in our thoughts, words and prayers. We trust Him as our most valued friend.
- We honour Holy Spirit as the person of God, entrusting ourselves to His leadership in whatever we do.
- We see ourselves as a beloved child of God, an heir to His inheritance of kingdom blessings.

Secret of the Hiding Place

Harmony in our soul brings peace to our heart. Our choice to place God first harmonizes our soul with Heaven's music.

Revelation from God

Recently in prayer I asked the Lord what He wants to reveal to us in the troubled times we are living in with wars, genocides against innocent people, extreme negative situations in the lives of most people (with health issues, financial hardships, injustices taking place that cause much grief, terrible losses from chaotic weather with storms, bushfires, earthquakes and so on). It seems as though the world and humanity is out of balance wherever you look. I believe that God is always in control and that all the suffering we see will end in His timing. We cannot give up hope that good will come in spite of all the evil manifesting itself on earth. The following is what I heard from God.

"The veil of deception is being lifted from those who have strayed from what Jesus accomplished on the cross. My Truth is stripping away those false idols humanity has placed ahead of the One True God, Yeshua. It is time for a Moses' encounter with God, time to place Him first, time for all the veils covering people's hearts to be ripped open, to reveal the pulsating beat of God's heart. It is time to connect our hearts to His heartbeat. All the things separating people from God are crumbling like the walls of Jericho as God's trumpets are now declaring: It is time to hear the sounds of Heaven's Truths being trumpeted over earth. It is time to connect our hearts to the sounds of Heaven, to declare God's glory with our mouths as we praise Him with all our heart, soul and mind for all to hear."

We live in serious times, where we cannot compromise who God is and what He is conveying to us. We must take a stand for righteousness, where God's glory is revealed (in right acts) by how we choose to live. His love is always available to everyone on earth. These are times where there is no room for grey areas (compromises) in our lives. As we allow God's light to shine through us, we become a lantern, where the fire of Christ within us is waiting to be set aflame through our faith, and acts of righteousness. This is how evil will be overcome.

Secret of the Hiding Place

The love of God dispels all darkness in its wake.

Scripture: James 1:17-18 (NLT)

"Whatever is good and perfect comes to us from God above, who created all heaven's lights. He never changes or casts shifting shadows. In His goodness He chose to make us his own children by giving us His true word. And we, out of all creation, became His choice possession."

EMBRACE GOD'S LOVE FOR YOU!

Give God space in your heart. How? By allowing Holy Spirit to heal your broken emotions, painful memories and fears of rejection, your shame, guilt, self-doubts and offenses against anyone who hurt you. We cannot overcome adversity in our own strength. God is our strength, and the more we turn to Him and depend upon Him to carry us through our difficult times, the greater our victories will be. Living in God's presence can become a lifestyle of being connected to Him through all our challenges. How do we establish such a lifestyle? Think of Holy Spirit as your source of life, the very breath you need to live. He is our spiritual life-blood that flows into our spirit in a continuous cycle of renewal. We connect with Holy Spirit by giving our heart to Jesus Christ. When we ask Jesus into our heart, a re-birth takes place in us, meaning we join ourselves to God through Christ. We are now connected to God's spiritual umbilical cord that feeds us everything He offers us. We are never separated from God's source of life; we can be distracted by life's demands upon us, but Holy Spirit never leaves us. We enter into deeper communion with God by consciously recognizing His presence in us. The more we focus on Holy Spirit by acknowledging Him in all our ways, the closer we draw to the heart of God. This is how "heaven invades earth" through us. The more we acknowledge our dependence upon God, the closer we become entwined with His love for us.

Why are we afraid of submitting control of our life to God?

In Western society in particular, striving for independence represents freedom. We are encouraged to compete for our value and self-worth. Submission to authority is considered weakness of character, and the loss of individual freedom. We have lost touch with the Godly values our way of life was built upon when our forefathers established democracy in our land. God was placed first in America's Constitution – "In God we trust!" These values were the roots of democracy that built the United States of America into the most powerful nation on earth. We may not be able to change nations, yet we can influence our personal world by choosing to place God first in our life. As we take a stand for God in how we live, we strengthen ourselves in kingdom values, which are kindness, goodness, unconditional love for others, tolerance, peace, justice and the pursuit of happiness for all. This is how the hidden power of God is released into our life. Do not be afraid of losing control of your independence by submitting to God. True freedom comes by doing what is right in God's eyes.

Scripture: Matthew 10:39 (NLT)

"If you cling to your life, you will lose it; but if you will give it up for me, you will find it."

What does this Scripture really mean?

Another way of saying we need to give up our life to find it is to say: We need to die to our old self. In an earlier chapter I wrote about what took place when Jesus died on the cross and was resurrected into eternal life, and what this means to each of us personally. Through Jesus' sacrifice of Himself for us, we now have Holy Spirit living in us as a free gift from God. In order for us to benefit from this free gift, we must *accept* it. This may sound obvious, yet many of us hold onto our old identity with all of its limitations, which prevents us from stepping fully into the new life Jesus gave us at the cross. Our old self is referred to in Scripture as our 'old man' before Christ entered our heart. Our 'old man' is what we are familiar with, including our thought patterns, our emotions, old habits and programmed responses in dealing with life's issues. Our brains have been formatted according to how we lived life up to this point in time, just like a roadmap or blueprint with established routes travelled in our past. We are creatures of habit who fall into familiar patterns of behavior, based upon what we learned from our past experiences. We sub-consciously accept these familiar patterns when defining who we believe we are. When we choose to follow Jesus, the challenge for us is to allow our 'old man' to die, so that we can be transformed into a "new creature" in God's image. How do we do this?

Firstly, we need to understand we *can* change when we are willing to do so. We begin this process by changing our beliefs about who we really are. This requires an open heart willing to turn away from who we believed we were. We have to *want* to change, regardless of how frightening this may seem as we choose to believe God. As we choose to face our fears and walk through them (rather than avoid dealing with them), we are creating a new roadmap for ourselves to travel in a more positive direction. We need to look forward by focusing on God's promises for us. As we choose not to look back at our old, familiar ways of thinking and acting, we make progress in our new journey with God. The more we take a stand for Truth, by refusing to settle for any kind of deception that keeps us from all the good things God promises us, the stronger we become. Dying to our old beliefs about who we thought we were is a process. The key to transformation is your willingness to allow Holy Spirit to reveal to you how much you are loved, cherished and valued by God. There is no need to strive in this transformational journey from your old self, to become a "new creature in God's kingdom." Position your heart towards Him and God will do the rest. As you choose to trust God in this process, your heart beliefs will change, so that your whole life will eventually be transformed. As you turn your heart to face the new dawn of each day, your past will recede into the background of your memories. Choose to begin each new day seeking God's guidance in your thoughts, words and actions. As long as you are facing God, you will be guided into all the good things He has for you.

The key to dying to our old self is our willingness to want God more than what is familiar to us.

Secret of the Hiding Place

Plug into your unlimited potential by aligning your thoughts with how God sees you.

Learn to listen to Holy Spirit!

We can 'tune in' to Holy Spirit by acknowledging His presence, by asking for help when we need it, by praying, worshiping and loving God, by opening our heart to 'hear' what He is saying to us. I wrote in earlier chapters of Brother Lawrence who lived in the 1600's. I refer to him because it is so easy to relate to this modest, humble man who recognized his need for God, and considered Holy Spirit to be his best friend. Holy Spirit is *our* best friend as well, when we allow Him to rule our heart. The key here is our willingness to submit ourselves to His leading. As long as we choose to overrule Holy Spirit's presence, by placing our opinions, desires and needs above His leadership, we will not 'hear' Him or experience His presence. As we follow God's will for us, we are drawn closer to who He is, resulting in us experiencing deeper levels of intimacy with Him, as He pervades our spirit. We find ourselves craving His presence in every detail of our life. We become aware that we are nothing without Him, and everything with Him. The tide of Living Water from Heaven sweeps over our soul, consuming the very essence of us as we connect with the heartbeat of God. This is a picture of what it means to live in "God's hiding place" within you, where you experience complete oneness with your Creator.

The following is an exercise to help you enter into God's presence.

Visualize yourself in this scene. Allow yourself in your imagination to enter into a glorious garden filled with huge evergreen trees, flowering shrubs, brilliantly coloured flowers lining the pathway you are walking along. You hear the sounds of exotic birds perched on the branches above your head, singing songs that deeply stir your heart. Butterflies of unbelievably beautiful colours are flitting all around you, some alighting upon you. The sunshine is filtering through the dark green foliage above you. A flowing brook of crystal clear water bubbles over stones in a nearby creek bed, creating a comforting sound of trickling water that soothes your soul. A majestic figure appears before you in a flowing white garment; His eyes rest upon you, filled with overpowering love and compassion for you. He reaches His hand towards you, beckoning you to place your hand in

His. You take His hand and are overwhelmed with a sense of joy and inexplicable happiness; you feel loved, cherished and valued, with the awareness you are being 'seen' for the first time for who you really are. You recognize that this is what you have always wanted and hungered for, but did not experience until now. You know you have entered into the presence of God, filling you with hope, purpose and the knowledge that you are "home." You are aware that you never need fear anything ever again. You have encountered Christ Jesus. You are in the atmosphere of Heaven. You have entered His "hiding place" where you feel safe, loved and complete.

This is who you really are and where you belong! As you live in this reality, you understand God is with you, whatever life brings your way from this time onwards. You have become a "new creature" (**2 Corinthians 5:17**), a pearl of great price. You are now on the road that will take you towards your true destiny.

Scripture: Numbers 6:24 (NIV) Prayer of God's blessings for you

"The Lord bless you and keep you;

the Lord make His face shine upon you and be gracious to you;

the Lord turn His face towards you and give you peace."

Amen.

REFLECTIONS

- Describe your understanding of who Holy Spirit is?

- What is our role in our relationship with Holy Spirit?

- Can you identify any 'props' you have relied upon that prevent complete surrender to God's will and intimacy with Holy Spirit living in you?

- Write a list of blessings you receive when you allow yourself to be guided by God's Holy Spirit.

- How do we connect with Holy Spirit?

- To help you answer this question, follow the suggestions given in this chapter.

- Think of some ways God's love can be embraced by you?

- Are there areas in your life you have difficulty submitting to God?

- Are you willing to surrender them to God?

- How do you learn to listen to Holy Spirit?

- Place yourself in the garden described in this chapter to receive God's unconditional love, peace, grace and comfort as you rest in your "Hiding Place" with Him.

NOTES AND RECOMMENDED READING

- A CHRISTMAS CAROL written by Charles Dickens. Published by Chapman & Hall, London in 1843. Movie Produced and Directed by Brian Desmond Hurst. Distributed by Renown Pictures – UK 1951.

- Movie A BEAUTIFUL MIND. Producer and Director: Ron Howard and Brian Grazer. Distributor: Universal Pictures and Dream Works Pictures in 2001.

- Book ALICE IN WONDERLAND written by Lewis Carroll. Published by Macmillan & Co. in UK 1865.

- THE HIDING PLACE written by Corrie ten Boom. Published by Bantam Books October 1, 1984 in the Netherlands.

- THE PRACTICE OF THE PRESENCE OF GOD with Spiritual Maxims written in the 1600's by Brother Lawrence. © 1958 and 1967 by Revell. Published by Spire Books, a division of Baker Publishing Group.

- SWITCH ON YOUR BRAIN © 2013 written by Dr Caroline Leaf. Published by Baker Books in Grand Rapids, Michigan, USA.

- STRENGTHEN YOURSELF IN THE LORD © January 4, 2007 written by Bill Johnson. Published by Destiny Image Publishers, Shippensburg, PA, USA.

- BECOMING THE PERSON YOU WANT TO BE – Printed in the United States of America © 2004 written by Dr. James B. Richards. Published by Milestones International Publishers, Newburg, PA, USA

- TAKE CONTROL OF YOUR LIFE © Dr. James B. Richards 2012. Published by True Potential Publishing, Travelers Rest, SC USA

- QUANTUM GLORY – The Science of Heaven Invading Earth © 2010 by Phil Mason. Published by XP Publishing in Maricopa, AZ. USA.

- THE MIRACLE OF WATER written by Masaru Emoto, MD © 2007 published by Beyond Words Publishing Inc. and Simon and Schuster Inc.

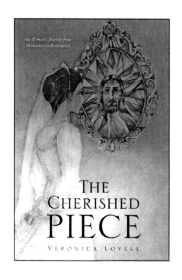

THE CHERISHED PIECE - Author Veronica Lovell

This previous book, written by Veronica Lovell, describes her journey from brokenness (through sexual abuse as a child), to God's restoration in her mind, emotions and spirit. The Cherished Piece teaches how forgiveness is the key to breaking free from any negative consequences from past trauma of any kind. You will be led towards inner healing and freedom, as Veronica's story encourages you to trust God in this process. Each chapter contains steps clearly laid out for you to follow, to enter into new hope as your identity is restored, so that in the end, you too will have your own testimony of how to step into everything God offers us when we follow His ways.